MANAGING
BUSINESS
IMPROVEMENT
AND QUALITY

MANAGING BUSINESS IMPROVEMENT AND QUALITY

Implementing
key tools
and techniques

BARRIE DALE
AND RUTH MCQUATER

First published 1998

2 4 6 8 10 9 7 5 3 1

Blackwell Publishers Ltd
108 Cowley Road
Oxford OX4 1JF
UK

Blackwell Publishers Inc.
350 Main Street
Malden, Massachusetts 02148
USA

British Library Cataloguing in Publication Data

A CIP catalogue record for this book is available from the British Library.

Library of Congress Cataloging-in-Publication Data

Dale, B. G.
    Managing business improvement and quality : implementing key tools and techniques / Barrie Dale and Ruth McQuater.
        p.   cm.
    Includes bibliographical references and index.
    ISBN 0–631–20787–2 (alk. paper). — ISBN 0–631–20788–0 (pbk.   : alk. paper)
    1. Total quality management.   I. McQuater, Ruth.   II. Title.
HD62.15.D348   1998
658.5′62—dc21   97–22300
                                                                        CIP

This book is printed on acid-free paper

Contents

List of Figures and Tables

Preface

The main focus of this book is how to use tools and techniques in an effective and efficient manner. In conjunction with colleagues Dr Ruth Boaden and Mr Mark Wilcox, the authors were involved in a successfully completed Engineering and Physical Sciences Research Council (EPSRC) funded project with the theme of 'Total Quality Management: Integration and Development'; we acknowledge the contribution of our colleagues to the material contained in this text. The work was carried out over a period of three years and involved collaboration with eighteen organizations on thirty-one manufacturing sites in the UK, the USA, France, Germany and Spain.

A major strand of the research was to assess the use of tools and techniques and how process owners made best use of them, in particular as part of their daily work activities. Among the issues investigated were the difficulties encountered by organizations in the application of tools and techniques and identifying the key influences that impact on their effectiveness and efficient use. It was the positive response to the findings of the project from the organizations collaborating in the research that provided the inspiration for the production of this text.

The evidence and material on which this book is based came from the work carried out on the above-mentioned research project and the subsequent preparation of two booklets in cooperation with TQM International. The material has been supplemented from a number of other sources, including:

- Research carried out by the UMIST Quality Management

Centre over a period of some sixteen years on a variety of quality management projects involving the use of tools and techniques.

- The operation of the UMIST Total Quality Management (TQM) Teaching Company Programme, which has been in operation from early 1987 and has involved thirty-four associates in twenty-eight different organizations.
- The coordination of the Rexam Industrial Packaging and RHP Bearings Ltd. Multi-Institute TQM Teaching Company Programmes, involving seven manufacturing sites, six universities and eight associates and five sites, four universities and seven associates, respectively. A number of the associates employed on these programmes have tackled two-year programmes of work involving the use of tools and techniques in practical situations.
- Training and practical experience of using tools and techniques, including the operation since 1984 of the Ford Motor Company Northern Regional Training Centre for training Ford's suppliers in statistical process control.
- Discussions with a range of practitioners, managers, trainers and consultants.

A considerable number of textbooks focus on individual tools and techniques such as design of experiments, quality costing, quality function deployment and statistical process control. On the other hand, only a handful give adequate treatment to a range of tools and techniques. Having said this, there are a number of booklets produced by management consultancies that serve to act as reference guides and *aides-mémoire* to the user of tools and techniques.

What sets this book apart from others is that it covers a range of tools and techniques, focusing not only on their description and construction but also on the difficulties, both general and specific, in their use and application. It also gives guidelines to the user to overcome the typical difficulties encountered. Case histories of good and best practice are outlined throughout the various chapters. Another unique feature of this text is the provision of a methodology, which can be used in self-assessment mode to assess the strengths and areas of improvement relating to the use and application of tools and techniques. The methodology was developed from the research project and has been trialed in a number of organizations in both the UK and continental Europe.

The book is targeted at the user of tools and techniques in

manufacturing, commercial, public sector and service organizations. In this respect, management at all levels of the organizational hierarchy, as well as the more technical and engineering based personnel, will find something of value in the book. Irrespective of the approach taken by an organization to TQM, a selection of tools and techniques will be required. All of the evidence that we have collected suggests that the use and application of tools and techniques is fraught with problems. Any management team interested in making best use of tools and techniques would benefit from studying the contents of this book. A conscious effort has been made to produce the text in language that is free from jargon.

MBA students and postgraduates studying courses involving TQM and continuous improvement disciplines will find the book of value, as will those studying for professional examinations or undergoing post-experience training involving these types of considerations. There is a growing number of undergraduate courses that involve elements of TQM, and students of such courses will find chapters 6 and 7 of particular use. These chapters outline in simple and clear terms the main tools and techniques likely to be used in a process of continuous improvement. The growing band of academics teaching and researching TQM should also find the book to be of help.

During the course of the research, we have learned a lot from our collaborating organizations. We consider that this book reflects this knowledge. In producing the text we have not set out to produce a weighty tome, but rather to distil, in summary form, the key learning issues in the successful use of tools and techniques. We believe that this aim has been met, and sincerely hope that you, the reader, concur with this view. However, any ideas for improvement will be warmly received.

Barrie Dale and Ruth McQuater
Quality Management Centre
Manchester School of Management
UMIST

1 The Role of Tools and Techniques in Total Quality Management

Introduction

Irrespective of the approach taken to total quality management (TQM), an organization will need to use a selection of tools and techniques to introduce, support and develop a process of continuous improvement. Some of these tools and techniques are simple (sometimes deceptively so), while others are more complex. Without the effective employment and mix of tools and techniques, it will be difficult to solve problems and make improvements. The various tools and techniques have different roles to play in a process of improvement, and, if applied correctly, give repeatable and reliable results. Their use helps to get the improvement process started and also assists in picking up the pace of improvement, often lifting the process out of a period of stagnation, thereby helping management to achieve business results. Employees using tools and techniques feel involved and that they are making a contribution, quality awareness at all levels of the organization is encouraged and enhanced, behaviour and attitude change is facilitated, and projects and problems are brought to a satisfactory conclusion. Organizations should always be on the lookout for how they might improve the effectiveness of the application of tools and techniques.

The purpose of this chapter is to introduce the reader to the concept and key elements of TQM and to examine the role of tools and techniques within that framework. It opens by examining TQM and its main elements, and traces its evolution. The importance of quality in a business context is discussed and the case for tools and techniques is made.

What Is Total Quality Management?

There are many definitions of TQM, and it is clear from the differences that the concept requires a disciplined business approach to be adopted. This is based upon a fundamental belief in the need for continuous and company-wide improvement, to understand and meet the requirements of customers, identify and build upon best practice, and be cost effective.

In today's markets, customers' requirements are becoming more rigorous and their expectations of the product/service in terms of its conformance, reliability, durability, availability, interchangeability, performance, features, appearance, serviceability, environment- and user-friendliness, and safety are also increasing. At the same time, it is likely that the competition will be improving in terms of products, technology, service, value for money etc., and new and lower cost competitors will emerge in the market-place. Once a process of improvement has been halted, under the mistaken belief that TQM has been achieved and the ideal state reached, it is much harder to restart the process, differentiate the organization's products and service, and gain the initiative in the market-place.

Starting a process of improvement and then developing and fostering its advancement needs to be a long-term organizational objective. It typically takes eight to ten years to put the basic principles into place, but respectable savings can be made within the first year, providing that the appropriate balance of inputs and outputs is achieved and key deliverables, such as resolution of problems, are emphasized. In TQM, there are no quick fixes; no single technique and/or tool that may be considered as a panacea for all ills, and similarly none is more important than another; no short-cuts; and no ready-made packages and programmes that can be plugged in to guarantee success. Continuous improvement requires patience, tenacity, understanding, skills and considerable commitment from people at every level in the organization, in particular the senior management team. Facilitators and champions are prerequisites and their role in continuous improvement cannot be overemphasized.

Much has been written by authors from a variety of disciplines on the importance of continuous improvement in the current economic climate. Whole businesses have sprung up concerning TQM implementation and what organizations must do and have, and the sequence of implementation and training that must be undertaken if TQM is to be successful. Most of what is articulated, particularly by the popular 'gurus', is often prescriptive in its origins and evangelistic in its approach. Throughout the past decade, numerous consultants and training organizations have jumped on the bandwagon of peddling the latest management fads. Typical of the examples that spring to mind are ISO 9000 series registration, statistical process control (SPC), benchmarking, self-assessment against a model of business excellence and business process re-engineering. There is potential, in these circumstances, for organizations to view these consultants' directives as a panacea that will cure all ills, but what is not recognized is that they often fail to provide any solid foundation for sustainable success and that those peddling the packages may lack the necessary knowledge and improvement skills. Unfortunately, management are often taken in with the glitz rather than the pragmatism. Underlining this is that despite many reported individual successes there are countless numbers of failures, not only of improvement initiatives but of other management systems and methods. It is also worth noting that while the majority of consultants are comfortable with the selling and application of prescriptively based 'packages', those with pragmatic and practical improvement skills are in short supply.

Despite the divergence of views on what activities comprise TQM, there are a number of common elements. These elements are now discussed. This material is based on Dale et al. (1994), and the practical and research experience of the UMIST Quality Management Centre.

Commitment and leadership of the chief executive officer

Without the total commitment of the chief executive officer (CEO) and his or her immediate executives, nothing much will happen on TQM, and anything that does will not be permanent. They have to take charge personally, lead the process, provide direction, exercise forceful leadership – including dealing with those employees who block improvements – and maintain the impetus. However, while some specific actions are required to give TQM a focus, it must be seen as the natural way of operating a business as quickly as possible.

Planning and organization

The facets of planning and organization include:

- Developing a clear, long-term approach, which is integrated with other business strategies and plans such as information technology, production/operations and human resources.
- Deployment of the policies through all stages of the organizational hierarchy, with objectives, targets, projects and resources agreed with those responsible for ensuring that the policies are turned from words into deeds.
- Building quality into designs and processes.
- Developing prevention-based activities (e.g. mistake-proofing devices).
- Putting quality assurance procedures into place that facilitate closed-loop corrective action.
- Planning the approach to be taken to the effective use of quality systems, procedures and tools and techniques, in the context of the overall business strategy.
- Developing the organization and its infrastructure to support improvement activities. While it is considered useful to set up some form of steering committee or council, to provide direction and support and to make people responsible for coordinating and facilitating improvement, the infrastructure must not be seen as separate from the management structure of the business.
- Pursuing standardization, systematization and simplification of work instructions, procedures and systems.

Using tools and techniques

Without the effective employment of tools and techniques it will be difficult to solve problems and increase the velocity of improvement. The tools and techniques should be integrated into the routine operation of the business, and a route map should be developed by the organization for the tools and techniques that it intends to apply.

Education and training

Employees, from the top to the bottom of an organization, should be provided with the right level of education and training to ensure that their general awareness and understanding of quality concepts, skills and attitudes are appropriate and suited to the continuous improvement philosophy. This also provides a common language throughout the business. A formal programme of education and training needs to be planned and provided on a timely and regular basis to enable people to cope with increasingly complex problems. It should suit and be relevant to the operational conditions of the business. For example, is training to be undertaken in a cascade mode (i.e. everyone is given the same basic training within a set time frame) or is it to be done as an infusion process (i.e. training by team/function on a gradual and progression basis)? The programme of education and training should be viewed as an investment in developing the ability and knowledge of people and helping them to realize their potential. Without training it is difficult to solve problems, and without education, behaviour and attitude changes will not take place. The training programme must also focus on helping managers to think through and identify what improvements are achievable in their areas of responsibility.

It also has to be recognized that not all employees will have achieved adequate levels of education. The structure of the training programme may have to incorporate some updating of basic educational skills in numeracy and literacy, but it must also promote continuing education and self-development. In this way, the latent potential of all employees can be released.

Involvement

There must be a commitment and structure to the development of employees, with recognition that they are an asset that appreciates over time. Employee interest and participation is essential to continuous improvement, and all available means – from suggestion schemes to various forms of teamwork – must be considered to encourage their involvement in the business. Management must also be prepared to share some of their powers and responsibilities. This involves seeking and listening carefully to the views of employees and acting upon their suggestions. Part of the TQM approach is to ensure that everyone has a clear understanding of what is required of them, how their processes relate to the business as a whole and how their internal customers are dependent upon them. The more people understand the business and what is going on around them, the greater the role they can play, and therefore business improvement is that much easier to make. People have to be encouraged to own, control, manage and improve the processes that are within their sphere of responsibility, but they must also have an understanding outside their own areas.

Teamwork

To be effective, teamwork should be practised in a number of forms. Consideration should be given to the operating characteristics of the teams employed, how they fit into the organizational structure and the roles of team sponsor, leader, member and facilitator. Teamwork is one of the key features of involvement and is helpful in gaining the commitment and participation of people throughout the organization. It is also a means of maximizing the output and value of individuals.

There is also a need to recognize positive performance and achievement, and to celebrate and reward success. People must see the results of their activities and be aware that the improvements they have made really do count. This is actively encouraged through effective communication. If TQM is to be successful, it is essential that communication be effective and widespread. Often managers can be good talkers but poor communicators.

Measurement and feedback

Measurement of progress, from a baseline, needs to be made continually against a series of key results indicators – both internal and external – in order to provide encouragement that things are getting better (i.e. fact rather than opinion). External indicators are the more important because they relate to customer perceptions of product and/or service improvement. The indicators should be developed from existing business measures, and external and internal benchmarking, as well as from customer surveys and other means of external input. This enables progress and feedback to be assessed against a roadmap, checkpoints or a model such as the Malcolm Baldrige National Quality Award (MBNQA) or the EFQM Business Excellence model. From these measurements action plans must be developed to meet objectives and to bridge gaps.

Working together

It is necessary to create an organizational culture that is conducive to continuous improvement and in which everyone can participate. Quality assurance and improvement practices also need to be integrated into all of an organization's processes and functions. This requires changing people's behaviour, attitudes and working practices in a number of ways:

- Everyone in the organization must be involved in 'improving' the process under their control on a continuous basis and must take personal responsibility for their own quality assurance.
- Employees must be encouraged to identify wastage in all its various forms.
- Employees must inspect their own work.
- Defects should not be passed, in whatever form, to the next process. The internal customer–supplier relationship (everyone for whom you perform a task or service or to whom you provide information is a customer) must be recognized.
- All people have to be committed to satisfying their customers, both internal and external.
- External suppliers and customers must be integrated into the improvement process.
- Mistakes must be viewed as an improvement opportunity.
- Honesty, sincerity and care must be integral parts of daily business life.

Changing people's values and attitudes is one of the most difficult tasks facing management, requiring considerable powers and skills of motivation and persuasion. Serious thought is required to facilitate and manage culture change.

The Evolution of Quality Management

The evolution of quality management can be traced through four main stages (Dale et al., 1994):

1 Inspection. 'Activities such as measuring, examining, testing or gauging one or more characteristic of an entity and comparing the results with specified requirements in order to establish

whether conformity is achieved for each characteristic' (BS EN ISO 8402, 1995).

2 Quality control (QC): 'Operational techniques and activities that are used to fulfil requirements for quality' (BS EN ISO 8402, 1995).

3 Quality assurance (QA): 'All the planned and systematic actions implemented within the quality system and demonstrated as needed to provide adequate confidence that an entity will fulfil requirements for quality' (BS EN ISO 8402, 1995).

4 Total quality management: 'Management approach of an organization, centred on quality, based on the participation of all its members and aiming at long-term success through customer satisfaction, and benefits to all members of the organization and to society' (BS EN ISO 8402, 1995).

The first two stages, inspection and quality control, are based on a detection approach to the management of quality. With this approach the emphasis is on the product, procedures, service deliverables and the downstream production and delivery processes. Consequently, considerable effort is expended on after-the-event inspection, checking and testing of the product and/or service and providing reactive 'quick fixes' in a bid to ensure that only conforming products and services are provided and delivered to the customer. The stages of quality assurance and TQM, on the other hand, are based on prevention, and concentrate on upstream activities in relation to product, service and process design. This evolution is shown in diagrammatic form in figure 1.1. This figure also shows some of the typical characteristics of each stage of evolution. These four stages are progressive and embracing: quality control embraces inspection; quality assurance embraces quality control; TQM embraces quality assurance.

It is only when an organization starts to change its approach from detection to prevention, with a clear emphasis on planning quality into the processes, that the use of tools and techniques is considered more seriously by the senior management team. This starts to surface when management become aware that their current approach to improvement is deficient and start to consider a more formal approach to problem solving. Prior to this it is usual to find that only a few simple tools, such as graphs and checklists, have been used. In other cases, techniques such as SPC have been used but because of limited understanding have been deployed incorrectly and/or the results misinterpreted.

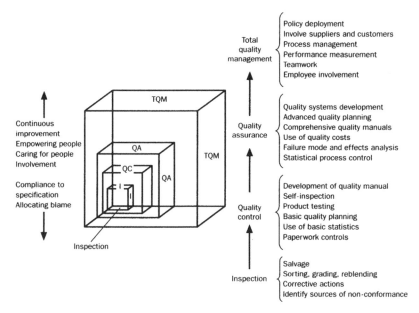

Figure 1.1 The four levels in the evolution of quality management. *Source*: Dale (1994)

The Importance of Quality in a Business Context

In the last decade many organizations have come to appreciate that TQM will enable them to become and remain competitive in both home and international markets. In many of these markets, quality, and its continuous improvement are now qualifying criteria. TQM not only leads to increased productivity, higher standards, improved systems and procedures, improved motivation and increased customer satisfaction but also to lower costs and bottom-line savings. It means quality at the most effective cost (i.e. value for money).

Today, quality is regarded by most producers, customers and consumers as crucial to their manufacturing, operations, service and purchasing strategies. To understand why, we need only recall the unsatisfactory examples of products/services we have experienced, how we felt about them, the actions we took, and the people we told about the experience and the outcome, if any. Waiting for a customer complaint is too late. Quality concerns and near misses need to be monitored to provide a mechanism for turning concerns into improvement opportunities and retaining customers and their loyalty. An organization should always be aware that niggling incidents can cause aggravation to the customer, and whenever a customer becomes dissatisfied, a loss of goodwill results. This leads to extra effort being expended by personnel within the organization, investigating what has gone wrong and then trying to put right that wrong. These unsatisfactory experiences result in actual costs above what has been budgeted, which have a direct impact on bottom-line performance and can also result in erosion of market share.

Following on from this an order, contract or customer lost on the grounds of non-conforming product and/or service quality is much harder to regain than one lost on price or even delivery grounds. The customer could be lost forever – in simple terms, the organization has been outsold in the market-place. If we doubt the truth of this statement, we need only consider the number of organizations that have gone out of business or lost a significant share of a market, and examine the reported reasons for this situation. Quality is one of the factors that is not negotiable. In today's business world, the penalties for unsatisfactory product quality and poor service are likely to be punitive. When the management of an organization compares its profit-to-sales ratio and its quality-costs-to-sales-turnover ratio, they will find that the cost of quality is of the same order as profitability. Dale and Plunkett (1995), based on a variety of companies, initiatives and situations, claim that the cost of quality (or, to be more precise, the cost of not getting it right) ranges from 5 to 25 per cent of an organization's annual sales turnover. This provides an immediate indication of the importance of quality to the business. Goodman and Adamson (quoted in Anon. 1993), estimate that:

> the cost of not meeting customer expectations to a British company manufacturing products which people buy several times a year, with each purchase producing a $25 profit, would be $1.5 million lost profit annually.

Kano et al. (1983) carried out an examination of twenty-six companies that won the Deming Application Prize between 1961 and 1980. They found that the financial performance of these companies in terms of earning rate, productivity, growth rate, liquidity and net worth was above the average for their industries.

A report published by the US General Accounting Office (1991) focused on the top twenty scorers of the MBNQA in the period 1988–1989. On the basis of a combination of questionnaire and interview methods, the companies were asked to provide information on four broad classes of performance measures: employee-related indicators, operating indicators, customer satisfaction indicators and business performance indicators. Improvements were claimed in all indicators. Useful information on financial performance was obtained from fifteen of the twenty companies, which experienced the following annual average increases:

- Market share: 13.7 per cent
- Sales per employee: 8.6 per cent
- Return on assets: 1.3 per cent
- Return on sales: 0.4 per cent

Larry (1993) reported on a study carried out on the winners of the MBNQA and found that they 'yielded a cumulative 89 per cent gain, whereas the same investment in the Standard and Poor 500 Stock Index delivered only 33.1%'. Wisner and Eakins (1994) also carried out an operational and financial review of the MBNQA winners, in the period 1988–1993. One of the conclusions reached was that the winners appeared to be performing financially as well or better than their competitors.

The US Commerce Department's National Institute of Standards and Technology (NIST) invested a hypothetical $1000 in each of the five publicly traded whole company MBNQA winners and the parent companies of seven subsidiary winners, and also made the same investment in the Standard and Poor's 500. It was found that these twelve companies outperformed the Standard and Poor's 500 by almost three to one. In addition, NIST also invested a hypothetical $1000 in a group of 32 companies receiving MBNQA site visits; these companies outperformed the Standard and Poor's 500 companies by two to one. Curt Reimann (1995), the director of the MBNQA programme at the time, commented on the results:

> This review adds to the mounting evidence that, done right, quality management can lead to outstanding returns in many business areas including financial performance, satisfied customers, and improved market share.

A study carried out at the University of Bradford Management

Centre identified twenty-nine companies within the UK that display characteristics associated with TQM (Letza et al., 1997). The study was first carried out over the period 1987–1991 and has been repeated for the period 1991–1995. Nine measures were used by the study team to compare company performance with the median for the particular industry. The second study revealed the following:

- 81 per cent of companies are above the industry median for turnover per employee
- 81 per cent of the companies provide a higher salary to turnover ratio than their peers
- 74 per cent of the organizations remunerate their employees above the median for the industry.
- 65 per cent of the organizations produce above median profit per employee for their industry
- 62 per cent of the organizations have a higher net asset turnover than their peer group

The authors also went on to say that 'Four of the nine measures are marginally below the median for their industry but this is to be expected as quality becomes institutionalised and more widespread.'

Aeroquip, which is a wholly-owned subsidiary of the Trinova Corporation, uses its own modified version of the MBNQA, called AQ+, for self-assessment. Worldwide, Aeroquip has 40 sites in twelve countries, employs nine thousand people, and is a global manufacturer of fluid power connectors and custom engineered plastic parts and assemblies. The president of the corporation has made it an objective that every site should achieve AQ+ by December 1996. This requires a score of 700 points. By the end of 1994 nine of the forty sites had met this requirement, and the following business data on these nine was produced by the corporate quality director:

- 64 per cent of Aeroquip operating income from 31 per cent of sales
- 15.1 per cent return on sales against 3.9 per cent for the rest of Aeroquip
- 21 per cent growth in sales compared with 5.0 per cent for the rest of Aeroquip
- 31 per cent growth in income compared with a 3.2 per cent decrease for the rest of Aeroquip

The most extensive study of the impact of TQM on corporate performance was provided by Easton and Jarrell (1996). They studied the impact of TQM on the performance of a sample of 108 firms which began serious efforts to implement TQM between 1981 and 1991. It was concluded that 'performance, measured by profit margin, return on assets, asset use efficiency, and excess stock returns, is improved for the sample of firms that adopted TQM.'

While there are methodological problems with most of these studies, the broad picture emerging is of the benefits of quality management competence in terms of competitive advantage and business performance.

The Case for Tools and Techniques

While there is clearly a good case for the use and application of tools and techniques, they are not a cure-all for every problem and must not be treated as an end in themselves. The bottom-line objective is their effective deployment in order to improve the performance of the business.

In superior performing organizations everyone is encouraged to use tools and techniques in a structured way as part of the problem solving process. They assist in managing by fact rather than by perception. It is recommended that an organization start with the more simple tools, such as check sheets, checklists, Pareto diagrams, cause and effect analysis and flow charts, and ensure that the tools and techniques currently employed are being used properly before attempts are made to introduce others. There are a considerable number of management tools and techniques (table 1.1) it is important that organizations do not rush headlong into the use of a plethora of tools and techniques. Customer pressure and contractual requirements can have a strong influence on the use of a specific set of tools and techniques. For example, some customers look to the use of techniques such as SPC and failure mode and effects analysis (FMEA), some to quality costing and mistake-proofing, and others to self-assessment. They may be what management believe the market-place will be expecting in the future. The view may also be taken that the use of a specific technique will give the organization an edge over its competitors. The tools and techniques in use may be what improvement teams have found to be helpful in solving problems.

Table 1.1 Commonly used tools and techniques

The seven basic quality control tools	The seven management tools	Other tools	Techniques
Cause and effect diagram/analysis	Affinity diagram	Brainstorming/brainwriting	Benchmarking
Check sheet/concentration diagram	Arrow diagram/critical path analysis	Control plan	Departmental purpose analysis (DPA)
Control chart	Matrix diagram	Flow chart/process modelling	Design of experiments/Taguchi methods
Graphs/charts	Matrix data analysis method	Force field analysis	Failure mode and effects analysis (FMEA)
Histogram/tally chart	Process decision programme chart	Questionnaire	Fault tree analysis (FTA)
Pareto diagram	Relations diagram	Sampling	Poka yoke (mistake-proofing)
Scatter diagram/regression/correlation	Systematic diagram/tree diagram		Problem solving methodology
			Quality costing
			Quality function deployment (QFD)
			Quality improvement teams/quality circles
			Statistical process control (SPC)
			Vendor assessment and rating

When selecting tools and techniques, there are three main factors that organizations should keep in mind:

1 The application of any tool and technique in isolation without a plan, framework and long-range management vision will only provide short-term benefits.
2 No one tool or technique is more important than another; they all have a role to play at some point in the improvement process.
3 The education and training requirements that underpin the effective use of the tool or technique should be given due care and attention.

A number of companies use tools and techniques without thinking through the implications giving rise to misconceptions and misunderstandings that eventually become barriers to progress. The evidence acquired from the UMIST research (e.g. Lascelles and Dale, 1993; McQuater et al., 1994) indicates that many companies attempt to use specific tools and techniques as the springboard to launch a process of improvement without giving sufficient thought to issues such as:

● How will it facilitate the improvement process?
● What is its fundamental purpose?
● What will it achieve?
● Will it produce benefits if applied on its own?
● Is it right for the company's product, services, processes, people and culture?
● Is the company being given the right advice?
● What organizational changes are necessary to make the most effective use of it?
● What is the best method of introducing and then using it?
● What are the resources, skills, information, training etc. required to introduce it successfully?
● Does the company have the management skills and resources, and the commitment, to make it work successfully?
● How will it fit in with, complement or support other tools, techniques, methods and systems already in place, and any that might be introduced in the future?
● What are the potential difficulties in its use?
● What are its limitations, if any?

It is important for managers to address such questions when considering the introduction of any tool or technique. Unfortunately, some managers are always on the lookout for tools and techniques as a quick-fix solution to the problems facing their organization at a particular point in time. In general, management teams that are 'technique reactive' tend to be unclear on the concept of TQM and continuous improvement. They often confuse the implementation of a particular technique with TQM and tend to use the technique as an end in itself rather than as a means to an end. A current case in point is the way in which some organizations are attempting to use, in prescriptive mode, self-assessment against a recognized business excellence model as the 'cradle to the grave' approach to TQM.

If the management team is preoccupied with specific techniques and lacks an adequate understanding of TQM, the major danger is that tools and techniques will be picked up and discarded as fashion changes, similar to a magician pulling magic balls out of the air or rabbits out of a hat (figure 1.2). When this happens and a tool or technique fails to meet expectations, disillusionment sets in and the company experiences considerable difficulty convincing its employees that it is serious about improvement. This, of course, has an adverse effect on the future use of tools and techniques in the organization. One of the main reasons why companies fall into this trap is that they have unduly high expectations of the benefits arising from the use of a single tool or technique. Much of this is a result of the publicity and selling that often accompany specific techniques. The use, on its own, of a single tool or technique will usually produce a small, incremental improvement. It is only as a result of the cumulative effect of tools and techniques used in series within an adequate framework that an organization will start to see some real long-term benefits from its improvement endeavours (figure 1.3). Therefore, organizations should resist the temptation to isolate the benefits arising from any one tool or technique.

The motivation for the use of any particular tool or technique is a key factor in the success of its implementation. Dale and Shaw (1990) reported that when a major customer insists upon the use of a specific technique as a contractual requirement of its suppliers, two phases can be identified in its use. Firstly, the technique is applied by the supplier to satisfy the demands of the customer in order to maintain the business. During this phase the supplier often resorts to a number of camouflage measures, fakes and

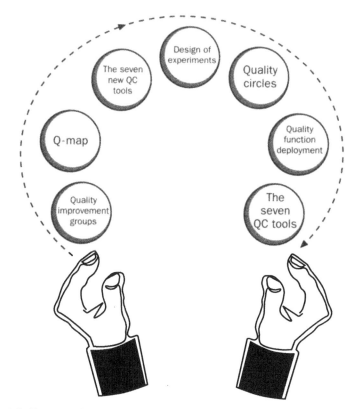

Figure 1.2 The use of quality management tools and techniques: the juggling approach. *Source*: Dale and Cooper (1992)

ruses to convince the customer that the technique is being applied in an effective and beneficial manner. The emphasis in this phase is on satisfying the customer's paperwork and quality system certification requirements. Dale and Shaw go on to make the point that this phase is wasteful in terms of time and resources, but suggest that suppliers sometimes appear to need this phase to develop their own awareness and understanding of the technique being applied. The second phase begins when the supplier's management team start to question how they might best use the technique to enhance the company's competitive position. This is when real improvements begin to occur. Dale and Shaw (1990) also point out that automotive component suppliers appear to have reached this second phase in a shorter period of time with

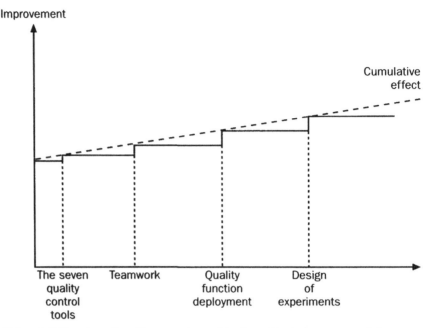

Figure 1.3 The use of quality management tools and techniques: cumulative improvement effect. *Source*: Dale and Cooper (1992)

FMEA than they did with SPC, and suggest that this is due to the learning experience. Those organizations using techniques such as SPC for the sole reason of satisfying the quality system audits of major customers are missing the direct benefits of the correct use of the technique and also the opportunity that it affords to make improvements. The danger in adopting this approach is that the improvement process goes only as far as the customer requires.

Evidence suggests that organizations do appear to go through phases in their use of a particular tool or technique. For example, Dale et al. (1997), describing a case study on Maxtor (HK) Ltd, report that the company witnessed three phases in its use of SPC:

1 The use of SPC in attribute mode (i.e. p charts) at the final inspection stage.
2 The use of SPC in parametric model (i.e. $\bar{X}$ and R charts) to measure key process parameters.

3 The use of design of experiments to identify the key process parameters.

Because of the variety of starting points and motivations for improvement, it is not possible to identify a universal implementation plan detailing the order in which specific techniques should be used by an organization, nor is it possible to tell managers what to do next with respect to their use of tools and techniques. However, one piece of advice that can be offered is that organizations should start with the simpler tools and ensure that these are used together in an integrated manner, with interchange of information between the tools. Simple tools and techniques can be just as effective as the more complex ones. In some organizations there is a tendency to ignore the simple tools, and those that are used tend to be applied in isolation, whereas the superior performing companies tend to use tools and techniques together and visibly display the results on a story board. In this way they are not only listening to the process through tools such as control charts and check sheets, but also taking action to improve. It is this combined use of tools that facilitates problem resolution and improvement action.

Summary

There is a need for greater industrial efficiency and competitiveness if the UK's manufacturing industries are to participate in the open markets not just of Europe but of the global market-place. However, an increase in efficiency alone will not automatically provide the means for greater competitiveness, since it requires that the product and/or service must satisfy the customer's requirements. This implies that the organization must be constantly improving the quality of both its products and its processes. To this end, many organizations follow the principles and philosophies of TQM, and intrinsic to TQM is the use of techniques and tools. They are a starting point in the study of a problem and are a key foundation block in the problem analysis and resolution processes. They help to identify, quantify and diagnose problems and gaps in performance. This entails educating and training the workforce in order that the techniques or tools be used effectively, thereby enhancing the continuous improvement process. If tools and techniques are not used in a structured way, people will tackle a problem and focus on the symptom but never get to the root cause and put in place long-term corrective action.

However, tools and techniques on their own are not enough; they need an environment that is conducive to improvement to facilitate their use. An organization's senior management team have a key role to play in the effective use of tools and techniques. They should, for example:

- Develop their knowledge of the tools and techniques and, when appropriate, use them in their day-to-day activities and decision making.
- Delegate responsibility for their promotion to suitable individuals.
- Maintain an active interest in the use of tools and techniques and the results.
- Endorse expenditure arising from the education and training required and the improvement activities resulting from the employment of tools and techniques.

The ideal stage for an organization to reach is one in which tools and techniques are such an obvious part of the problem solving process that people use them naturally.

2 Tools and Techniques: An Introduction

Introduction

Many of the tools and techniques discussed in this book are themselves not new and have been around for many years in one form or another. In some cases they are nothing more than old concepts wrapped up in new clothes. However, no matter how they are dressed up and presented, tools and techniques are practical methods, skills or mechanisms that can be applied to particular tasks and assist with the solving of problems. In our experience tools and techniques are frequently used in many different contexts, often without people realizing it. For example, graphs and charts employed by staff in an administrative function are data presentation tools; similarly, an informal use of failure mode and effects analysis (FMEA) is often practised by engineers and technical specialists in their day-to-day work activities. The crucial factor is how to make best use of tools and techniques and ensure that they are used regularly and consistently to facilitate continuous improvement within a structured framework.

As outlined in chapter 1, for the majority of organizations embarking on an improvement process, the use of tools and techniques is the initial thrust of the approach. In many cases the only training given to the majority of people in relation to TQM is related to tools and techniques, yet their use is not as widespread and effective as might be expected. This approach more often than not involves creating quality improvement teams who are trained to work on specific problems, which in turn call upon the use of tools and techniques to solve problems. However, in many firms the use and application of tools and techniques do not make the transition from team-based activities to everyday deployment by individuals in the processes for which they are responsible (e.g. from the boardroom to the shop floor and office, and by the sales force out in the field). When proper training of tools and techniques is undertaken coupled with people who are capable of making improvements, and with the right motivation, the potential for resolving problems can be considerable.

This chapter examines what is meant by tools and techniques and considers why their use is important to a process of continuous improvement. The role of tools and techniques is also explored, along with where and how to use them.

What Are Tools and Techniques?

In this book the term 'tools and techniques' is used generically to describe practical methods and skills applied to particular tasks to facilitate change and improvement. It is clear that there is considerable variation in what people perceive as tools and techniques, what each tool or technique comprises, and its perceived role and potential value to the improvement process. There are also differences in the terminology used to describe tools and techniques, and the methodology of their deployment. In some cases different names are used to describe very similar tools and techniques, and vice versa. There is also little attempt to distinguish between a tool and a quality technique. Dale et al. (1993a) have proposed the following definitions of tools and techniques.

> A single tool may be described as a device which has a clear role and defined application. It is often narrow in its focus and can be and is usually used on its own. Examples of tools are:
>
> - Cause and Effect Diagram
> - Pareto Analysis
> - Relationship Diagram
> - Control Chart
> - Histogram
> - Flowchart
>
> A technique, on the other hand, has a wider application than a tool. There is also a need for more intellectual thought, skill, knowledge, understanding and training to use them effectively. A technique may even be viewed as a collection of tools. For example, Statistical Process Control employs a variety of the tools such as graphs, charts, histograms, and capability studies, as well as other statistical methods, all of which are necessary for the effective use of the

technique. The use of a technique may cause the need for a tool to be identified.

Examples of techniques are:

- Statistical Process Control
- Benchmarking
- Quality Function Deployment
- Failure Mode and Effects Analysis
- Design of Experiments
- Self-assessment

Why Use Tools and Techniques?

Tools and techniques play a key role in TQM. When used effectively, they:

- allow processes to be documented, monitored and evaluated,
- encourage everyone to become involved in the improvement process,
- encourage people to be persistent and to ask basic questions,
- assess the performance of the process and highlight problem areas,
- allow people to solve their own problems and take a closer look at what is happening,
- facilitate the development of a mindset of continuous improvement,
- provide the means of transferring experiences from improvement activities to everyday business operations,
- reinforce teamwork through problem solving,
- make a contribution to the achievement of business results,
- provide a framework which ensures that the right things are done first time and every time,
- assist in visualizing data,
- produce countermeasures to abnormalities, and
- provide the means by which teams and individuals can demonstrate and measure the progress they are making towards TQM.

Tools and techniques require attention to be paid to a number of 'critical success factors' to make their use and application both effective and efficient. These include:

- full management support and commitment at all levels of the business. Management and staff should be fully aware of the main purpose and use of the tools and techniques they are considering applying,

- effective, timely and planned training,
- a genuine need to use the tool or technique,
- defined aims and objectives for its use and a planned approach to application,
- an environment that is conducive to improvement,
- available and accurate data, including the appropriate means and methods of measurement,
- backup and support from improvement facilitators,
- tools and techniques in current use must be employed effectively before attempts are made to introduce others,
- the temptation to single out one tool or technique for special attention should be avoided,
- the limitations of how and when tools and techniques can best be used should be understood, and
- tools and techniques must be used as an integral part of the business operations.

When the critical success factors are in place, the use of tools and techniques provides a means to:

- define the issues that are important to the business,
- identify the root causes of problems,
- develop, test and prototype solutions, and
- implement a permanent solution and build this, as appropriate, into procedures.

Organizations appear to have difficulties in selecting appropriate tools and techniques and then getting them to work effectively, in particular getting people to use them in their day-to-day activities. These difficulties often arise because some or all of the critical success factors are missing.

It is essential that a problem solving methodology is introduced, as part of the process of continuous improvement, alongside tools and techniques, to provide a framework for their effective use. There are many such problem solving methodologies and frameworks (e.g. Ford Motor Company, team orientated problem solving (TOPS), eight-discipline (8D)) but they all have a number of common steps:

- identify the opportunities for improvement,

- define, in quantitative terms, the opportunity to be tackled,
- evaluate all the possible root causes and select the most likely, and
- act to implement and follow up the solutions.

The Use and Application of Tools and Techniques

There are a variety of means for classifying the tools and techniques used in a process of improvement. Tools and techniques can be broadly categorized as relating to (1) role, (2) tasks and activities associated with the improvement process, and (3) the stages/steps involved with a process of improvement.

Tools and techniques have a variety of roles to play in improvement, both of a specialist and universal nature. In a number of cases the individual tool or technique also fulfils more than one role. This applies in particular to techniques. Thus, it is not surprising that there are no definitive guidelines on the primary roles played by each tool and technique. Despite the potential confusion, users must always be aware of the main uses of the particular tool and technique they are considering applying. These uses include:

- collection of data
- summarizing data
- presentation of data
- discovering problems
- selecting problems
- understanding a problem
- assisting with the setting of priorities
- finding and removing the root causes of a problem
- identifying relationships
- structuring ideas
- performance measurement
- capability assessment
- planning
- implementing actions
- monitoring and maintaining control

Table 2.1 shows a typical classification of tools and techniques, aligned to their main perceived role, and table 2.2 shows a categorization of quality management tools and techniques.

Table 2.1 Role of quality management tools and techniques

	Roles	*Tools and techniques*
1	Checking	Checklists, control plans
2	Data collection/presentation	Check sheets, bar charts, tally charts, histograms, graphs
3	Setting priorities/planning	Pareto analysis, Arrow diagrams, Quality costs
4	Structuring ideas	Affinity diagrams, Systematic diagrams, Brainstorming
5	Performance/capability measurement/assessment	Statistical process control, Departmental purpose analysis
6	Understanding/analysing the problem/process	Flow charts, Cause and effect diagrams, Process decision programme charts (PDPC)
7	Identifying relationships	Scatter diagrams/regression/correlation, Relations diagrams, Matrix diagrams
8	Identifying control parameters	Design of experiments
9	Monitoring and maintaining control	Mistake-proofing, Failure mode and effects analysis, Matrix data analysis
10	Interface between customer needs and product features	Quality function deployment

Source: Dale et al. (1993b)

By answering the specific questions given in table 2.2 for each tool or technique, it will readily be apparent where each one resides along the simple/complex spectrum. To illustrate the point, brainstorming is considered simple in concept, application and understanding of how to use it by team members. It is tactical in its application and provides a sound structure that can be followed easily. On the other hand, it involves a strategic assessment of competitiveness, the impact on specific processes can be considerable, cross-functional teamwork is a necessity if its findings are to be applied effectively, and data collection can be complex, in particular when it involves outside organizations.

Table 2.2 Quality management tool and technique categorization

	General category	Specific questions to be considered

1	Roles of the tool or technique in the improvement process
	Expectations and objectives for use
	Understanding:
	   senior management
	   middle management
	   first-line management
	   operators/staff
		What is the tool/technique's main role?
		What other roles might it have?
		Why should it be used at this time?
		Is this the right application for it?

2	Organization and infrastructure
	  Commitment, support and :
	     encouragement
	     senior management
	     first-line management
	     operators/staff
	Allocation of resources
	Involvement of appropriate
	  staff and functions
	Training
	Communication
	Timing and rate of introduction
	System and environmental issues
		Who needs to be involved in the use of
		   the tool/technique?
		What organizational structure is needed?
		What support/equipment/resources are
		  needed?
		What training is needed?
		Is training to be one-off or ongoing?
		What standard definitions are necessary?
		What changes in culture are necessary?

3	Data collection
	  Time required
	  Knowledge and skills
	  Terminology
	  Preparation, format and
	    construction
	  Recording and consistency of
	    data
		Who is involved?
		What is required?
		How often should data be collected?
		How is data to be collected?
		What is the best format?
		Where is data collected?

4	Tool/technique use and
	    application
	  Ownership and response
	  Integration with other tools
	    and techniques
	  Use of the data
	  Flexibility of tool/technique
	    applications
		How and where is the data processed?
		Are the data processing mechanisms
		applicable?
		What are the outputs from the
		tool/technique?
		Who uses the outputs?
		When/how often are the outputs used?
		Why are the outputs used?
		Where is the tool/technique most
		  applicable?
		What other tools/techniques should be
		  used in combination?

Source: Dale et al. (1993b)

Where to Use Tools and Techniques

In the majority of organizations tools and techniques are commonly used to solve problems, undertake projects, demonstrate commitment and facilitate improvement. They are used in the majority of the processes of a business but in some cases on an ad hoc basis, in particular by those farthest removed from the manufacturing/operations function. The achievement of a positive outcome from an improvement activity can provide the impetus for the continued use of tools and techniques. Everyone, including managers, should be encouraged to use tools and techniques as a matter of routine in their business activities. Within an organization, all employees should be able to:

- find a use for tools and techniques in their processes,
- find opportunities to make improvements and cost savings, outside of quality improvement teams, and
- improve the effectiveness of the tools and techniques currently used.

Summary

This chapter has provided an introduction to tools and techniques. In particular, it has explored what tools and techniques comprise, an argument has been made for their use and their role within a process of continuous improvement. Tools and techniques are generic terms that refer to methods that can be applied to both product service, and process quality. They are a cornerstone of continuous improvement. Having both specialist and universal applications, they are as many and varied as the people and organizations that use them. However, if they are not used in a systematic manner, improvements are likely to be random and spontaneous rather than consistent and comprehensive.

It is difficult to imagine how any problem can be solved effectively without the use of tools and techniques. It is important that a general set of tools and techniques is identified for use within an organization and people trained to use them. As business needs develop, additional tools and techniques need to be identified and then applied. The point has been made that unless these types of issues are clearly thought out by those using tools and techniques there are likely to be difficulties encountered in their usage. This applies, in particular, in suiting tools and techniques, to specific situations and making best use of them.

The chapter has also examined a number of success factors that help to ensure the most effective application and deployment of tools and techniques. The issues aired in this chapter are examined in more detail in subsequent chapters.

3 Difficulties Encountered in the Use of Tools and Techniques

Introduction

There are numerous examples in the technical literature of the successful implementation of techniques such as SPC and FMEA, across different industries. Similarly, there are examples of the application of complex techniques such as design of experiments. There has also been discussion of difficulties and issues associated with the use and application of specific tools and techniques. However, little work has been undertaken to determine whether or not the issues and difficulties outlined are unique to an individual technique or tool or are found across all of them. This is an important consideration since problems surrounding their selection, use and application are not always addressed to the satisfaction of the people and organizations using them.

This chapter examines the difficulties and issues encountered in the use and application of tools and techniques.

Common and Specific Difficulties: An Overview

Based on an examination of a number of tools and techniques, Dale et al. (1993b) outline the common and specific difficulties and issues and their findings are summarized below.

The difficulties and issues relating to *all* tools and techniques include:

- resources
- management commitment
- detection-based mentality
- knowledge and understanding
- resistance to change

Management do not always make available adequate resources to facilitate improvement activities arising from the use of tools and techniques. A related issue is that management are unsure what they want from the tools and techniques that are being applied. Breaking the cycle of firefighting and transferring the resources used in detection to more front-end activity is not something that comes readily to management in traditional businesses, and to do this management commitment and leadership are necessary from the very top of the organization. This form of management support is more crucial with those tools and techniques that have a company-wide application (e.g. SPC, cause and effect analysis, brainstorming, Pareto analysis) than in the case of the more specialized tools, such as FMEA, design of experiments and QFD. Management commitment can, however, be superficial – for example, training on a particular technique, tool or set of tools and the outlining of future intentions for use being undertaken just to pass a customer's Supplier Quality Assurance assessment and to meet its contractual requirements.

The effective use of any tool and technique is dependent upon users' understanding and knowledge of it, their confidence and ability to collect data and carry out the appropriate construction, use it and interpret the results. The training process is a determinant in assisting with the transfer of appropriate knowledge, and some organizations have developed champions for particular tools and techniques. There is some value in doing this, especially where benefits for all concerned can be demonstrated.

In some organizations it is a common practice to create 'teams' (e.g. SPC teams) relating to the responsibility for the application and effective deployment of a specific tool or technique. This is dangerous. A better approach is to identify the root cause of the problem and then develop countermeasures, which may invoke the use of particular tools and techniques.

Any tool or technique imposes a certain set of disciplines. This discipline and procedure is difficult for some people to accept, with the result that they will deliberately misuse a tool or technique to prevent its effective use. The effective application of any tool and technique depends on using it in an honest and open way.

In addition to the difficulties associated with the individual's resistance to change, there is also the issue of the organizational environment. This can be considered as a cause and effect relationship. Typical causes include insufficient time, inadequate resources, incorrect timing of the application, customer pressure, and inadequate and inappropriate training. The effects include lack of acceptance, poor understanding and lack of use. These difficulties can be considered from a psychological angle – different personality traits lend themselves to different data collection methods – and from a sociological stance – the consequences for employees (e.g. job security, job satisfaction, pressure on time and increased decision making).

The issues relating to *specific* tools and techniques include:

- statistical knowledge and analytical skills
- expenditure
- visual versus static profile
- project-based training
- development of TQM

Difficulties in organizing, data collection and use relate to some tools and techniques more than to others. Those tools and techniques that require more than an elementary knowledge of statistics and a degree of analytical skills will encounter the most difficulties in acceptance. The tools and techniques that are used at the operating level of the business can highlight difficulties with literacy and numeracy at these levels. Those techniques such as QFD which require significant amounts of data gathering and analysis before results can be produced will encounter difficulties in their effective use. If results are not seen quickly, people will become impatient and will tend to switch their attention to what they claim are more pressing activities. Techniques such as design of experiments, which appear to be more complex than they actually are, require overcoming the lack of confidence in the potential user before they will be seriously considered.

The more complex techniques (e.g. QFD and design of experiments) require a certain amount of 'up-front' expenditure in terms of training and time away from the job. Many organizations are looking for a quick payback from the investment and this is not possible with such techniques.

Tools and techniques in which a visual display is part of their use (e.g. SPC, check sheets, Pareto analysis and cause and effect analysis) exhibit dynamism that tends to lead to an enhanced local ownership for their use. Consequently, they tend to encounter less difficulty in application than those which are less visible and portray a more static profile (i.e. FMEA).

Project-based training, using live examples, is a necessity to fully understand techniques such as FMEA, QFD and design of experiments, whereas with, for example, SPC and cause and effect analysis, a series of examples, often not directly applicable to a participant's business, will serve to illustrate their key characteristics. Providing these live examples is not easy for trainers and they often resort to more general training, with a consequential loss of effectiveness.

Some tools and techniques can be used with reasonable effect regardless of the development of TQM within the organization, but others will not yield effective results unless the TQM approach is well thought out and institutionalized. Until the organization is able to utilize the results of the tool or technique and translate them into improvement targets and actions, the technique or tool will not have been used to its full potential.

It is clear that many of the issues and difficulties, both common and specific, encountered with tools and techniques relate to:

- how and when they are taught,
- how they are understood,
- lack of skills and knowledge,
- incorrect application of the acquired knowledge,
- believing that they do not apply to managers,
- using them without a framework,
- using them without a purpose or aim, and
- misinterpretation of the data.

There are also several themes that contribute to any difficulties identified. They include:

- poorly designed training and support,
- being able to apply what has been learnt,
- inappropriate use of tools and techniques,
- resistance to use of tools and techniques,
- failure to lead by example,

- inadequate measurement and data handling, and
- not sharing and communicating the benefits achieved.

These are explored in the following subsections.

Poorly designed training and support

It is usual that training in tools and techniques succeeds quality awareness training. It is important that the design and delivery of such training is planned with the competency of the trainees in mind. This issue is examined in detail in chapter 4. In the case of courses held externally to the company the delegates are likely to experience a problem of transferring the new knowledge gained while on the course and applying it effectively in their own working environment. Any such course will only have the potential to change the attitudes of individuals, whereas delegates on return to their company have to motivate and change the working practices, attitudes and direction of both their peers and senior management. It is common for them to experience resistance from their company cultures.

Supervisors, technicians, quality management specialists and engineers tend to use tools and techniques more comprehensively than line operators, junior members of staff and even senior managers. These different categories of personnel require different levels of training. This is an important consideration when deciding the level of training required, the type of delivery and learning methods and even the trainer to be used. These types of factors will have a clear influence on the effectiveness of a training event or course and subsequent application. A difficulty faced by a number of organizations is that they train people in the tools and techniques in a way that does not always result in their regular and successful application in everyday aspects of the business.

Some points of guidance that may help an organization to improve its training are:

- Identify the tools and techniques that are considered to be most appropriate and of greatest benefit to the function.
- Train when there is a definite need.
- Demystify the learning process.
- Train people as and when they are expected to use a specific tool or technique (i.e. adopt a 'train' and 'do' approach).

- Consider the training requirements of specific individuals in the use of particular tools and techniques.
- Assess what prior knowledge those to be trained have and their basic level of numeracy and literacy.
- Choose the trainers carefully; check their credentials, knowledge and experience, and their ability to convey information to others.
- Ensure that the training sessions allow sufficient time for hands-on use of the tools and techniques; this will help to reinforce understanding.
- Ensure that a consistent message is given in the training.
- Be sympathetic to some people's, in particular, line operators', potential dislike of being trained in a classroom situation.
- Use practical examples from within the organization to reinforce the immediate relevance of a tool or technique.
- Practise the specific tool or technique on a real issue affecting those attending the training.
- Do not provide too much information in any one training session.
- Provide after-training support.

In relation to this last point, it should not be expected that once a person has been trained he or she will use the tools and techniques naturally without ongoing support. This support and reinforcement should include:

- basic application guidelines in lay person's terms,
- facilitators, trainers and immediate managers being available to coach, counsel and encourage individuals and teams to remember and use the tools and techniques they have been taught,
- team leaders trained and counselled to coach and lead their teams,
- provide suitable opportunities for individuals to use the tools and techniques in their everyday work processes through the use of controlled projects.
- follow-up practical sessions to reinforce the skills learnt, if possible in a workshop environment,
- provision of physical space and equipment (e.g. room, flipcharts, whiteboards, visual aids etc.) in a convenient area where people can meet to discuss and practise the use of the tools and techniques,

- evaluation of the effectiveness of the training given, including an assessment of the trainer, and improvement as necessary,
- showing how the tools and techniques can be used routinely as part of everyday business operations,
- evaluation of how the tools and techniques are being used in the workplace, and
- ensuring that new employees receive the appropriate skills training as early as possible.

Being able to apply what has been learnt

Even if the training and support are effective, there is often a reluctance by teams and individuals to apply what has been learnt. This usually has the dimensions of:

- lack of vision about when to use a particular tool or technique and its purpose,
- inappropriate use of tools and techniques,
- lack of confidence to apply the tool or technique to the processes for which they are responsible,
- lack of a structured approach and clear objectives that are communicated throughout the organization,
- lack of perceived benefit,
- tools and techniques being used in isolation rather than in combination, and
- perceived shortage of time due to production/operational pressures.

When learning anything new, the key to successful use is understanding how and when to use each new skill. Even when using a simple tool such as cause and effect analysis, it is important to understand when to use it and the role it plays. On the other hand, it should be remembered that it is not always necessary to use tools and techniques in order to make improvements. They should be used when the situation demands it, and in these circumstances support and encouragement from both facilitators and managers are essential. In addition, tools and techniques should be adapted to the situation for which the application is being considered. One very effective way of providing more clarity of vision is to ensure that the application and use are made within an improvement framework.

An example of the application of control charts in a first-line automotive component manufacturer highlights the above points. Many of the control charts in use contained up-to-date information, the data plotted was responded to with clear actions, and the operating staff had a good understanding of both the process and the mechanics and interpretation of the charts. However, in other sections and manufacturing cells of the same plant the control charts showed out-of-control conditions, with no apparent action being taken in response to the special causes of variation and statistical violations. In general, operatives knew their own processes and products, but did not understand how to apply the control charts. This also applied to the use of p (proportion of units non-conforming) and u (non-conformities per unit) charts. These were meticulously maintained but the information on some of them was indecipherable, because of insensitive and inappropriate scales. Other charts of the same type displayed data points indicating zero defects, when this was not the case. These types of problems underline several issues:

- ineffective coordination of the collected data
- limited understanding of how to set up charts
- limited understanding about the interpretation of data
- lack of analysis
- ineffective facilitation by management

Tools and techniques can be used individually for the routine pursuit of improvement, for problem solving and for other 'daily activities'. They can be – and are more often – used in a formal improvement team context. When this occurs, the teams should follow a structured approach which guides them to identify root causes and develop permanent solutions. There are several such problem solving approaches or processes. For example, the Quality Service Action Teams of National Westminster Bank (1987) use a six-step process of:

- selecting the problem
- identifying the causes
- investigating the problem
- developing solutions
- determining the action plan
- presentation to management

In the team member manual, members are also given guidance on which tools and techniques are appropriate to each stage of the process.

Another example is the Ford Motor Company (1991) Team Oriented Problem Solving Process, which provides a disciplined approach for solving problems and a reporting format to ensure consistency of use throughout the organization. The process follows a sequence of events, which is followed to the identification and subsequent resolution of a problem. It involves the following disciplines:

- using a team approach
- describing the problem
- implementing and verifying interim containment actions
- defining and verifying root causes
- verifying corrective actions
- implementing permanent corrective actions
- preventing recurrence

The following are the key features of a typical structured approach to problem solving:

Stage 1: Project proposal
- Identify:
  - team leader
  - team members and their training requirements
  - clear ownership/responsibilities
  - statement of problems and objectives
  - means of measuring progress
  - targets/milestones/project phasing/timescale/plan of action
  - communication needs
  - authorization to proceed

Stage 2: Step-by-step problem analysis
- Identify possible causes
- Investigate and develop a corrective measure to the abnormality
- Analyse and identify root causes
- Identify possible solutions to the problem
- Select and test solutions

Stage 3: Education, training and communication
- Involve all those likely to be affected by the problem and its solution
- Listen and respond to the feedback
- Consider education and training needs in relation to the proposed change(s)

Stage 4: Implementation planning
- Identify planned activities and the critical path of key actions
- Identify measures and ensure that the requirements are fully resourced
- Involve and train those affected by the solution

Stage 5: Implementation and follow-up
- Ensure that the solution is implemented
- Measure the improvements, assess the saving and check that the project objectives have been met
- Put in place follow-up actions, as necessary
- Report and communicate on success

Inappropriate use of tools and techniques

The inappropriate use of tools and techniques can be one of the more difficult areas to correct, and this introduces an additional set of obstacles to their effective use. It is extremely difficult to persuade someone who has recently been trained that the trainer has put across concepts and methods that are, in some way, flawed and based on outdated thinking. Unfortunately, this is on the increase, with the development of software for quality management applications. In a number of cases it is evident that those developing the software have a limited understanding of the concepts underpinning continuous improvement, and the implications and interpretation of the data generated by the program.

For example, in a Swiss plant involved in the manufacture of precision bearings the management team claimed that the process capability indices of their machines were around 0.2. This claim was made without the aid of control charts being displayed on the machines. Subsequent investigation revealed that key features of completed bearings were automatically inspected and the data gathered was fed into a computer package which generated a host of statistical data. Among this was data relating to cpk values and defect rates. A typical case of the output generated by the package was a cpk value of 0.21 and a defect rate of 99.85 per cent. Management, because of a fundamental lack of understanding of SPC, did not appreciate the absurdity of this data and the fact that the package was calculating process capability despite the lack of an assessment of whether or not the process was in a state of statistical control.

Having been taught a series of new skills, the temptation may be to use them all of the time. There will always be times when the improvement being targeted is so clearly obvious that the action required may be simply to do what is considered to be right at that time.

Three symptoms of the inappropriate use of tools and techniques are:

- Using tools and techniques to avoid making decisions. This is more common with managers and supervisors, who may be looking for excuses not to implement the obvious.
- A belief that 'we have used all the tools and techniques, therefore the improvement project must be successful'. The important factor here is that the tools and techniques are a means for people to use their knowledge and skills, and are only one part of the problem solving and improvement process, not an end in themselves.
- The data generated by the tool and technique, because of poor and inappropriate application, being used to draw incorrect decisions and develop misconceptions about the reality of the situation under study.

The most effective way to overcome this type of problem is to ensure that the training includes time to practise and understand the use of the tools and techniques that have been taught, reinforced by ongoing support that is sympathetic to the needs of the user. Users should always be encouraged to assess the results they are getting from the application of a specific tool or technique and, in particular, to challenge the designers and installers of computer-aided software used for tool and technique applications. However, it must not be forgotten that not all people have the ability or are willing to question any particular application – the 'do as you are told' syndrome.

Resistance to the use of tools and techniques

In many organizations, even after training, there can be a strong resistance to applying tools and techniques to the processes for which the trainees are responsible. The resistance usually increases as you move up the organization and in the more technical functions. One possible reason for this is that what are seen to be simple approaches are believed not to be relevant to management or to resolving issues related to technical development. Research and practical experience have shown that they are just as valuable, if not more so, to these types of situations. Managers in non-manufacturing functions should be particularly alert to this issue. Any such resistance may have its roots in:

- lack of familiarity with use
- concerns about numeracy and literacy
- use not being encouraged by managers and supervisors
- roadblocks put in place
- no process or framework to indicate which tool or technique to use and when
- people not given time to use them
- embarrassment at having to stand up in front of a group of colleagues or managers to present findings
- difficulty in breaking the firefighting cycle
- perception that the solution is already known and using tools and techniques will be too bureaucratic and slow
- lack of purpose
- 'another management fad'
- 'mickey-taking' by colleagues
- perceived excess control being exercised by management

If any of these symptoms are present in an organization, the main route to a solution will probably be in managers and supervisors being encouraged to use the tools and techniques themselves, and asking others to do the same. This may involve managers auditing and assessing the application of tools and techniques. The symptoms are usually more common when the tools and techniques are seen as specific to improvement and not employed in general everyday use. It is important to encourage managers and supervisors to use them in their regular meetings or when discussing issues with their own people. Here the emphasis should be on showing how and when they can be used, and the benefits that result from application.

Failure to lead by example

Leading on from the previous difficulty, it can be said that tools and techniques are not used as often as they should be by managers or as an integral part of the way they manage the business. Tools and techniques are perceived to be the province of improvement teams, only to be used when tackling projects and solving problems.

To ensure that the effective use of tools and techniques becomes a way of organizational life, it is essential that managers lead the way by using them in the processes and procedures for which they have ownership. Once they have done this they can then encourage others in the organization to do the same for their own processes. The following guidance may be of assistance:

- Managers are trained first.
- Managers use tools and techniques in their everyday jobs: 'do as I do!'.
- Develop a policy that includes recognizing and celebrating the success of those employees who make improvements through the use of tools and techniques in their everyday jobs.
- Promote those employees who practise and encourage continuous improvement.

Inadequate measurement and data handling

Tools and techniques are the key to developing a fact-based approach to problem solution and prevention. It is not uncommon to find tools such as process flow charting or cause and effect analysis being used to solve technical problems, but the transition to using them for people- or process-related problems is fraught with difficulties. The key aspects of this are:

- Do managers encourage measurement?
- Are individuals capable of handling and presenting data?
- Are measurements taken correctly?
- Is variation within the measurement system controlled?

Many organizations use measurement routinely in evaluating production performance, and for issues relating to stock control and financial management. However, measurements are still not effectively used routinely in a proactive approach in pursuit of continuous improvement. The acid test is to ask the question: 'how many times do we find ourselves firefighting?'. Management controls need not be used as a measure of failure but as a measure of success (e.g. 'how much more can be achieved, having got this far?' and 'what are our main strengths and areas for improvement?'). Using tools and techniques in this context is the key to improvement, and management reinforcement of the use of measurement in this way will encourage their use. For example, in a German automotive component supplier a considerable amount of resources had clearly been put into producing very colourful bar charts and graphs, giving a breakdown of deliveries from suppliers. However, because they carry so much information, such charts are incomprehensible to the uninformed. Although it may seem appropriate to plot all of the available data on one chart on many occasions, less is often more meaningful. This detail emphasizes 'the biggest is best' attitude, which is not necessarily the most effective approach to adopt.

With respect to the measurement of data, it is not uncommon to find that the operator's use of measuring equipment is not tested and measurement data is fudged. For example, in a first-line automotive supplier producing fabricated parts it was found that a measuring head employed to take the measurements of a critical component feature was manipulated by the operator exerting different degrees of pressure to achieve a measured value that was within the control limits on a mean and range control chart. This accounted for the low average range value and resulted in a false sense of security in terms of process performance and capability.

The desire to use tools and techniques may highlight difficulties that some individuals experience with basic numeracy and literacy. Although these difficulties are most often encountered at lower skill levels, it is not inconceivable to encounter them at higher levels in an organization. It is important to identify this as an issue within the organization and undertake basic training to tackle it. This can include:

- basic arithmetic and communication skills that are organization-specific
- data collection methods (e.g. check sheets, control charts)
- data handling techniques (e.g. means, ranges, standard deviations)
- graphical presentation (e.g. histograms, graphs, pie charts)

Not sharing and communicating the benefits

Nothing breeds success like success. One of the simplest ways of encouraging people to use tools and techniques in their day-to-day work activities is to share the benefits and successes with others in the organization.

Providing practical case studies of the effective use of tools and techniques helps to provide a means of recognition for those who have been involved in a successful application. Some practical ways of doing this include:

- Creating a database of examples within the organization, to which everyone has access.
- Building these examples into future training courses.
- Inviting individuals who have used the tools and techniques to present a summary on what they have done during a training session, particularly those examples of use in everyday business activities.
- Regular communication of successful use in company newsletters, on notice boards, as part of team briefings and during plant tours by customers and other visitors to the company etc.

Summary

The use of tools and techniques by organizations is by no means problem-free. There are many tools and techniques that may be applied to many different situations and for many different reasons. It is this variety, and their inherent complexity, that often creates difficulties in the selection, application and effective use of tools and techniques. In many organizations the techniques and tools at people's disposal will not be used to good effect. This is usually revealed by the amount of firefighting that takes place. The reasons for this cannot be explained in simple terms. There is a combination of factors, requiring extensive knowledge of the process, product and the techniques and tools being used. The effective use of tools and techniques is also related to the perception of their benefits by the user. This chapter has aired such difficulties, along with ideas for overcoming them.

4 Key Influences on the Use of Quality Management Tools and Techniques

Introduction

There are a number of 'success' factors in the effective use and application of tools and techniques, including a planned approach to implementation, management support and commitment, employee participation, and a well-designed education and training programme (Dale et al., 1997). From this research it was determined that these 'success' factors could be grouped into four broad categories: (1) role of the technique or tool in the improvement process, (2) organization and infrastructure of the company, (3) data collection, and (4) use and application of the technique or tool.

When linked to the four-part success classification, all of the information points to the fact that each category is subjected to various influences. These were determined as experience, management, resources, education and training (McQuater et al., 1994). Hence, it is the effects of these influences that cause the issues and difficulties associated with quality management tools and techniques, as illustrated in figure 4.1. An influence is defined as one causal factor having an effect on another, which then exerts an influence on the process and/or individual. Individual factors in each of the categories may not have an effect in isolation, but their accumulation causes a cascade effect, which then can exert a profound influence over the effectiveness of any given technique or tool, as shown in figure 4.2. This chapter examines these five influencing factors of experience, management, resources, education and training.

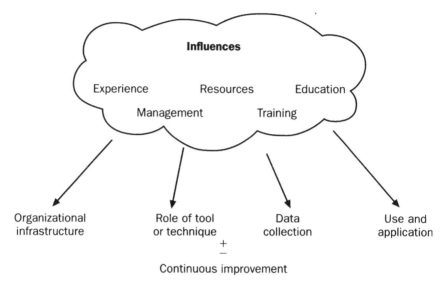

Figure 4.1 The effects of influences on continuous improvement

Experience

The length of time that an organization has been following a TQM initiative and its subsequent use of tools and techniques reflects on its ability to apply them to different situations and functions. Often the use of tools and techniques starts out as being driven by customer requirements. For example, the Ford Motor Company has, as part of its contractual conditions, placed requirements on its suppliers to implement SPC and FMEA. Under these conditions it has been found that 'lip-service' is often paid to their use, with organizations becoming adept at producing camouflage measures to satisfy the paperwork requirements in order to pass the customer's quality system assessment (Dale and Shaw, 1991). However, there is often a second phase during which they start to examine how they might use the techniques more effectively to aid their internal process of continuous quality improvement (Dale and Shaw, 1990).

Within any organization knowledge and experience of TQM and associated tools and techniques vary considerably among personnel at all levels of the organizational hierarchy. Often when some

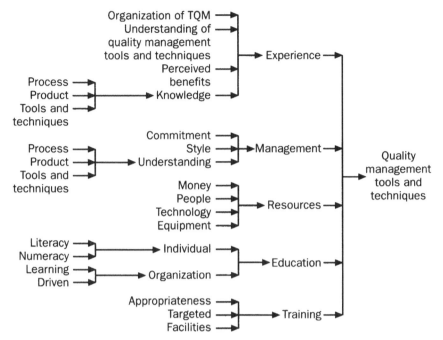

Figure 4.2 The cascade effect of specific influences on quality management tools and techniques

form of improvement initiative is being followed, the employees are aware of that particular initiative, but may fail to make the conceptual link to TQM. They may also fail to understand that, for example, self-assessment methods such as those based on the EFQM and MBNQA models of business excellence are merely frameworks for the introduction of TQM principles. To overcome this problem, improvement facilitators are often employed to act as emissaries to ensure that the message reaches all members of the workforce.

Lack of experience in both TQM and tools and techniques can cause fear and suspicion among the workforce, particularly when the potential benefits have not been made apparent to them. This is not entirely due to a lack of experience, knowledge and/or training, but is also due in part to the fundamental human distrust of change. If employees do not perceive any benefits of TQM or tools and techniques to their own working environment, do not understand why change is occurring, why a technique is being used or how to apply it to their processes, then they tend to pay only lip-service to the requirements of change and view organizational motives with mistrust. This can lead, at worst, to a breakdown in the TQM initiative, and, at best, to a failure to use the required technique or tool effectively.

Effective use of tools and techniques can help employees to accept more ownership for process improvement and decrease the amount of firefighting. The extent to which involvement takes place is also dependent upon leadership and communication. The use of the techniques and tools, as part of an advanced quality planning methodology, can provide clear indicators of the underlying causes of variation and how processes are performing.

Knowledge of tools and techniques and the understanding of them are entwined – without one, the other cannot be achieved. There are some techniques and tools that are best suited to data presentation or problem solving and others to the monitoring and evaluating of processes. Even in organizations well versed in the use of tools and techniques, there is still some hesitancy in consistently putting into practice what is known. This cannot be explained easily. It is not simply a lack of perceived benefits, although this can be the case, nor is it a lack of understanding of either the process, technique or tool. It is a combination of all factors and influences requiring knowledge of the process, product and the technique or tool being applied. The issue here is that the effectiveness of any technique or tool is dependent on how it is used, and how the application of it is supported and facilitated in the workplace. This point is well illustrated in an automotive component manufacturer. In common with many other organizations, it has contractual agreements with its customers to produce SPC information and documentation (e.g. process capability indices greater than 1.66), which in many cases demonstrated clear evidence that processes were in control. The operators, in this instance, showed a good understanding of both the process and the technique. However, in other areas of the same plant the control charts showed out-of-control conditions. No apparent action was taken in response to the special causes of variation or statistical violations, nor were the control limits based on the latest performance of the process. The operatives knew their own processes and products but did not have a good understanding of SPC. This was despite considerable resources being devoted to SPC training, including an interactive video disc system. Therefore, successful implementation and application of tools and techniques requires communication and cooperation at both the micro- and the macro-levels in the organization. This example also illustrates the requirement for facilitators to support, direct and maintain contact with users of the technique.

On a more positive note, Benneyan and Chute (1993) have shown that by becoming familiar with a tool or technique (in this case SPC), a group was stimulated into looking for new applications for it as a way of understanding processes and subsequently improving them, illustrating the importance of familiarity and experience of the technique in providing the impetus to apply it to new situations.

Management

Teamwork is an essential element of TQM, but because of long-established working practices and prejudices it is sometimes difficult for people to change their behaviour and attitudes. This can create many problems with respect to the use of tools and techniques. These barriers become more apparent when personnel from different functions are required to interact with each other, and are particularly noticeable when the process of continuous improvement is still regarded as being the domain of the quality department by both its staff and others within the organization. Consequently, there is a reluctance to assume responsibility for problems arising not only in production but also in other functions of the business. However, when departmental barriers are broken down and people identify their internal customers and attempt to understand and meet their requirements, the synergy created enables the organization to become more efficient.

Changing working practices and improved teamwork ought to enhance the empowerment of employees. However, difficulties can arise in getting line operatives to accept responsibility, particularly when there is fear and suspicion of management's motives. Other factors that can be seen as obstacles are the influence of unions, in both UK and European organizations, and, on the other hand, the reluctance of managers to relinquish what they see as their power base. Barriers can be eliminated, however, by involving all interested parties in the change process. In respect of these issues, it is not simply a matter of having a disciplined approach but rather of support and encouragement, with more structured and effective multi-channel communications.

There are strong indications suggesting that many difficulties exist in maintaining and sustaining effective use of tools and techniques, particularly when they are a contractual requirement of the customer. This suggests that employees are not fully committed to their use within their routine processes. Whether this is due to a lack of trust from managerial positions is uncertain, but it does suggest a failure to utilize worker knowledge of the process, with a lack of understanding displayed by the operators of the technique and a failure to be convinced of the benefits arising from its deployment. It is suspected that a combination of events and circumstances prevails. This will continue to be the case until managers demonstrate the necessary commitment to and leadership of TQM and the use of tools and techniques, and until workers develop sufficient skills and understanding to take ownership for the quality assurance and continual improvement of their own processes.

Most writers on the subject of TQM are agreed that any drive for change must be supported by top management. In some of the organizations studied it was found that if the senior management team were not sufficiently committed to continuous improvement, the process would eventually run out of steam. Similarly, if the strategy for continuous improvement conflicted with other company strategies or policies, such as those for manufacturing, marketing or financial aspects, and unless there was a senior executive driving the quality policy, it quite often failed to meet its objectives (Wilcox et al., 1994).

At the micro-level, many managers have embraced TQM with dedicated enthusiasm, and perceive it as the mechanism for the business to remain competitive. However, there is still a tendency for some of them to 'manage' TQM rather than lead by example, thereby stifling worker involvement. This is more noticeable in bureaucratic, hierarchical organizations where communication tends to be unidirectional with little cross-functional interaction, such as those found in the German and French plants that have been studied. This was manifest at operator level; operators tended not to be involved in the introduction and development of the improvement initiative, and saw quality as being the responsibility of the managers, with the use of tools and techniques as just another management ploy to keep them in check.

The root of this type of difficulty may be found in the education and training of all levels of the workforce. For change to occur, particularly from traditional value-based systems, improved general quality awareness training is required. In terms of tools and techniques, without management understanding, commitment to their use or support of those charged with using them, they tend not to be used effectively. Managers do not need to know the details and mechanics of any given technique or tool but they must be aware of its potential benefits, what to look for in its use, what questions to ask, and how to interpret and use the data. They also need to be aware of the application of tools and techniques and the sort of results that can be expected.

In order for quality to be integrated into production activities a greater degree of empowerment of operating staff is required. To facilitate this some organizations have removed a number of the responsibilities for quality (e.g. inspection) from the quality department and integrated them into the production process. However, this is not always clear cut. For example, in the same plant of a UK automotive component manufacturer there were two quite different management styles for integrating improvement into the manufacturing functions. In one division it was under the jurisdiction of the quality department, whereas in the other it was the responsibility of the manufacturing manager. In each division there was an SPC facilitator to ensure compliance with procedures and to support operatives in the use of SPC and other tools and techniques. It was apparent that more difficulties and conflicts of interest arose in the division where the responsibility for quality was with manufacturing. This is a direct contradiction of what might be expected in these circumstances. Usually when quality is placed under the auspices of production, a direct influence may be placed on process control and improvement, whereas when it remains the domain of the quality department there is a potential for lack of support from the production function to initiate change and take responsibility for quality assurance and improvement. One explanation for this is that placing the responsibility for quality in the hands of manufacturing adds to the dilemma of managers. During periods of work intensification and increased production volume, when customer demands become challenges, data collection and analysis are more likely to be at the discretion of the managers and supervisors, and may be seen as a low priority compared to meeting production schedules and satisfying the demands of customers.

Paramount to the successful introduction and effective use of tools and techniques is a champion – a person whose enthusiasm and knowledge can be used to good effect. This role may be filled by managers, provided they have sufficient knowledge, although it is more usual to seek out a motivated member of the front-line operating staff and train and coach him or her to the required standard. However, this enthusiasm and expertise counts for little if there is no managerial support or credibility, and particularly when there is a conflict between the production and quality functions.

Not everybody involved with the manufacture of products holds all of the information and has the necessary expertise. To illustrate this point, if, for example, there is no direct communication between the design engineers or the technical department and the production department, specific information and feedback will undoubtedly be lost. Therefore, to use tools and techniques effectively, open and honest communication between the functions is necessary, and this is the responsibility of management.

Resources

Resources in the context of this discussion refers to money, people, facilities, technology and time.

It is important that organizations ensure that whatever resources are at their disposal are used effectively and efficiently. Company employees are aware that pressure is being exerted on them from both internal and external customers, who want conforming products at the lowest price and demand the product and/or service when it is convenient to them. The demands of the customer dominate today's economic environment. A case in point is customers who are now demanding not only just-in-time supply but rather instantaneous delivery. This type of situation is described by a major American-owned first-line automotive component supplier as 'more for less and more for less' (i.e. improved quality, faster deliveries, more input into the customer's design process for a lower price per piece).

Few companies have been left untouched by the last recession, although most now appear to have weathered the storm. There are still many difficulties ahead, particularly for European organizations, with the threat from low-cost skilled labour from the former Eastern Bloc countries. A majority of organizations recognize that their greatest resource is their workforce, which needs careful selection, development, maintenance and utilization. It is their motivation and therefore cooperation that is essential to the effective working of any organization.

The fight to remain competitive during the recession has forced restructuring, a rationalization and downsizing of entire workforces. In some instances, whole hierarchical layers have been removed, usually at supervisory and middle management levels. The objective is to produce flatter, leaner and more effective workforces, but in many instances this can also increase stress levels. Consequently, this may have demotivating effects due to uncertainties about personal job security and organizational stability, in particular when the changes have not been well communicated. The effect of this is that employees can become uncooperative and demand unrealistic compensation for adopting the changes (for details see Mehrman and Harris, 1993). Discussion of leaner organizations by Skorstad (1994) has gone further by suggesting that reorganization leads to intensification of work, which in reality leads to a loss of autonomy. Rather than economies being made, they become diseconomies, with low efficiency, higher costs, and lack of worker commitment and involvement, in the form of restrictive actions. On the other hand, what many companies have found is that the positive outcomes of downsizing and resource restraints have allowed their workforces to concentrate their efforts in other ways, which actually complement the TQM philosophy – that is, making use of people's own expertise and enthusiasm by bringing their knowledge into the workplace. This was illustrated by a group of workers in a German automotive component manufacturer. They employed a 'poka yoke' philosophy to develop a rack and pulley system to facilitate component handling. This was not carried out during company time, but at home in their garages. In many such instances where tools and techniques are used in such a creative manner, workers may not know what to call the technique being used, its correct terminology or even that they have employed a tool or technique. What they are doing is working as a team to benefit their own working environment, which ultimately has a positive impact on the organization. Since there is nothing like success to convert sceptics, it is important to acknowledge communication and celebrate such innovations. Some people advocate token awards of recognition but in many instances a simple 'well done' note from the director responsible for the area is sufficient reward.

A further example of resource utilization is training key people in tools and techniques, and then using them to filter this knowledge to others in the organization. This can work very effectively but has its own set of problems. The people selected must be able to communicate this knowledge to others, be effective coaches and champions, and be seen as credible within the organization. They also require sufficient knowledge of the process and product, a clear understanding of the tool and/or technique to be employed, and the strength of character and authority to ensure that conformity to the set procedure is maintained and use made of the data collected to ensure that improvements do take place.

Facilities and resource allocation

The use of tools and techniques tends to generate large amounts of data, the analysis and interpretation of which can be daunting. The first problem is actually recognizing what is useful and what should be disregarded. This is by no means easy, particularly when customers require that specific information on products is to be kept for defined and often lengthy periods of time. This period is often dependent upon the industry and product. An obvious way of handling and storing data is to have a detailed filing and controlled documentation system, but it is easy for personnel to become swamped with data, which they find difficult to use because of its sheer volume. There is little point in collecting data if it is never analysed for trends and used to facilitate improvement, or if there is a problem with its coordination and exchange with people and functions. This was apparent to such an extent in several of the organizations studied that the duplication of quality improvement team activities had occurred on more than one occasion. This problem was overcome in other organizations with the provision of notice boards/story boards, placed in strategic locations throughout the plant. These included lists of teams, their membership, dates of when projects started, completion dates and a brief summary of the outcome. Similarly, documentation was listed for current projects.

Education and Training

To achieve the aims and objectives of TQM, effective utilization of the workforce is necessary. To this end, their education and training in quality awareness and the use of tools and techniques become priorities. However, employees do not have to become proficient in the more complex techniques, such as FMEA or design of experiments. If they can understand how to use basic tools, such as cause and effect analysis, control charts and check sheets, others can be learnt in time. A set of basic tools when used together provide a systematic and disciplined approach to problem solving and it is important that an organization has an education programme in place for such tools. If they are not used, focus tends to remain on the symptom, with the root cause of the problem rarely addressed and a failure to put into place long-term preventive actions. In many cases, the use of tools and techniques encourages operators to take a closer look at what is happening, instead of just reporting that there is a problem. The rationale behind their use is that they can teach operators to be persistent and ask questions of the process, thus expanding their knowledge of the underlying issues.

The dilemma facing the training manager is determining the organization's education and training requirements as opposed to those of an individual. For example, the organization as a whole has to be educated in improvement matters with appropriate training that can be presented to suit the person from an average educational background, but for an individual who has difficulty with even basic literacy, this would be inadequate. Having said this, the type of basic tools mentioned above are an essential training element in the continuous improvement process, in particular the training of personnel involved in quality improvement type teams.

There are very large differences in the education levels of workforces throughout Europe, as recent studies by writers such as Bierhof and Prais (1993), Mason and Wagner (1994) and Steedman et al. (1991) have shown. There are different skill levels available to employers, particularly at craft and intermediate levels. This has a direct bearing on how the workforce must be educated to suit the ever more demanding requirements of modern technologies and methods of manufacture. One of the limiting factors on the use of the more complex and more mathematically based tools and techniques is the educational standards of the people using them. In the UK in particular there has been a change in emphasis over the past two decades in the secondary education system, shifting from a skills and application base to a problem solving, conceptualization forum. This, along with the demise of company apprenticeship schemes and traditional technical education, may have a direct influence on how tools and techniques are used in manufacturing, and could have very serious consequences for the future competitiveness of the UK industries in particular, and continental Europe in general.

This is particularly emphasized by how information and knowledge are transferred. That is, a great deal of information and knowledge is transferred tacitly by watching and listening. This differs from the one-off approach of cascade, top-down training where the manager learns and then passes the explicit information on to colleagues or subordinates. It is rare for this sort of information transfer to progress from the explicit to the tacit (Baumard, 1996). For the sustained use and application of tools and techniques the underlying knowledge and information that support them must become tacit, and this can only happen if knowledge transfer is consistent, constant and sustained over time. This opens up the debate for lifelong learning and places particular emphasis on the manner in which the fundamentals of quality management are taught and how to achieve it at more fundamental and elementary levels.

Training in tools and techniques must not be carried out on an ad hoc basis. It should be carefully planned and implemented one stage at a time. There is little to be gained by training all people in FMEA, for example, when only a proportion of them can actually apply it to their own jobs or functions. In a similar vein, training should be timely, to coincide with the implementation of tools and techniques, and not when it is convenient for the trainer or even the organization. This is wasteful of both resources and skills, since by the time it is used the fundamentals will be forgotten.

Comparative analysis: Germany and the UK

The two plants described in the following discussion are wholly owned by an American corporation producing automotive components. In order to ensure a uniform approach to TQM the organization used a company-wide quality management self-assessment method based on the MBNQA. Although the German plant was somewhat behind its UK sister plant in the development of TQM, they faced some common difficulties and issues but, as the comparative study shows, also highlighted issues that were unique. This serves to illustrate the difficulty faced by global organizations when transposing common TQM strategies and policies across manufacturing facilities.

The analysis of data obtained from the UK and German sister plants highlighted several issues, including differences in workforce skills that may alter the effectiveness of tools and techniques. These effects on productivity and therefore competitiveness in different manufacturing markets have been well documented, by Mason et al. (1994) and Mason and Wagner (1994). Thus, one question that the comparative study investigated was the effects of these different skill levels on the use of tools and techniques.

There is a wide disparity in workforce skills in the two plants, with a pronounced difference in Germany at the lowest skill levels. This is due in part to a high percentage of imported labour, mainly from Turkey and the former Yugoslavia. In both these countries compulsory education falls short of the ten or eleven years of the UK and Germany. The result of this is that some of the workforce have difficulties with basic literacy and numeracy, which are necessary for them to learn not only the more complex techniques such as SPC, but also the simple tools such as histograms, cause and effect diagrams and Pareto analysis.

The nature of the job is a major determinant in the actual use of tools and techniques. In both plants the majority of the manufacturing processes require very little skill other than manual dexterity. Since data analysis and the sampling regime were carried out and determined by an SPC facilitator and/or quality engineer, the operatives were only required to collect data. In these circumstances they do not need even to understand SPC or its application, simply because they can rely on others to do it for them. There were few instances of members of the manufacturing cells or work teams taking responsibility for data interpretation and therefore control of the processes. There are several possible reasons for this, including inadequate compulsory basic education, which provides the foundation for understanding the training they have received in any particular tool or technique. Other reasons include perceived benefits in the communication of why a particular technique or tool is being used. The latter point must be emphasized for the reason that it is essential that communication and cooperation between the shop floor and management be maintained to get the data collected correctly in the first instance.

At lower to mid-skill levels in both plants the understanding and use of the more mathematically based techniques and tools varies considerably, which cannot simply be associated with educational differences, but may be more to do with tacit knowledge. The German plant plans to build quality into its products by using a variety of engineering methods, including some very complex mathematical modelling, and manufacturing conformance to design requirements is controlled through detailed and strictly applied quality assurance procedures. Therefore, its personnel have, in particular at a technical level, a deep grounding in statistics and quality assurance procedures. However, when making the conceptual step from assuring product quality to continuous improvement they appear to be experiencing some difficulty in applying techniques and tools. This may be put down to several things relating to familiarity, understanding, hierarchical structures, functional organization etc. On the other hand, the UK plant has experienced less difficulty in applying tools and techniques, despite the differences in workforce skills. Thus, although education and workforce skills play a major role in the ability of people using them, they are just one issue among many that affect the use, selection and application of tools and techniques and it is a major concern of organizations to address the issues in order that the best solution be obtained.

Although the comparative case study was carried out in one German plant, discussions with European quality managers from other organizations have supported the empirical findings. What is apparent is that the same influences do apply but they have a different emphasis. For example, German management styles and value systems are based on formality and control. The introduction of TQM into such settings calls for a far greater degree of flexibility and worker empowerment, which to some managers is akin to a loss of control and respect, bordering on anarchism. Despite the very strong technical tradition of producing highly engineered superior products, a great weakness in this structure is the apparent hostility to cross-functional cooperation. On the other hand, the British management culture thrives on flexibility, delegation and team working, although this too may be detrimental since it often manifests itself in crisis management, firefighting and 'macho' management.

From this case study the crucial point is that until organizations become aware of their own environment and culture there will be a continued tendency to ignore the influences that not only affect the use of tools and techniques but also affect other organizational issues in both administration and production.

Summary

There are critical success factors involved in the use of tools and techniques, which are subject to many internal and external influences. What emphasis these will have individually depends on the organization, its size, its business and the stage reached in the continuous improvement process. For example, small organizations have all the same training requirements as larger ones, but the allocation of resources may be the major issue. Similarly, the consequences for organizations of ignoring or being unaware of the influences affecting the use and application of tools and techniques could be potentially damaging, not only to the quality initiative in terms of cost, through investment in the initiatives, but ultimately to their competitiveness in the common market-place.

It is essential for companies to identify the nature of the influences operating both internally and externally, since failure to do so will inhibit the improvement process. This may be done in different ways, using a variety of audit methodologies. Whatever the method used, the information gained should allow organizations to identify their own problem areas and therefore address them by whatever means are at their disposal. Such a methodology is given in chapter 8.

For global organizations, identification of local influences has become almost essential for transposing corporate quality policies; failure to do so could have serious implications for the implementation and sustaining of the initiative. The point being made is that what works well in one country may not necessarily be successful in another. Similarly, with differences in education and training, corporate bodies must be aware of any discrepancies that may arise at the operating level of the business. Involvement of personnel at the different locations then becomes essential in the identification of specific needs and requirements. Such involvement serves two purposes. Firstly, personnel normally removed from the decision making processes play an active role in the quality initiative. Secondly, and perhaps more importantly, it provides evidence of organization commitment and support, particularly if grassroots suggestions are implemented successfully.

5 Implications for Education and Training

Introduction

Many of the difficulties encountered in the use and application of tools and techniques as outlined in chapter 3 can be put down to poorly designed and inappropriate training courses, failure to follow-up the training, and inadequate coaching of the trainee in the workplace to ensure that the tools and techniques that have been taught are put into use. A related education and training difficulty is a failure to take account of the trainee's basic education background. Organization and workforce profiles can have a profound effect on the utilization of tools and techniques, so it is important to determine these profiles prior to carrying out any training. It should also not be forgotten that tools and techniques create knowledge and this itself has implications for education and training. TQM is not a theoretical subject; it is a dynamic phenomenon, requiring practice to develop understanding and hone skills, and this is most relevant to the eduction and training requirements related to the successful use of tools and techniques.

This chapter discusses the rationale behind current quality-related management training policies and their relationship to workforce skills. It also includes a discussion on the learning needs of the organization as opposed to those of the individual.

Training

Education and training are basic tenets of TQM. The objective is to continually develop an individual's skills, and in this way enhance the skill base of the workforce. Training is often carried out in a vacuum, with little thought being given as to how the training that is provided can assist the process of improvement. There is little point in training without clearly specified improvement objectives.

The training should be specific, targeted and have a defined purpose. At an individual level, education and training are important to facilitate employee development and job satisfaction. This is evident from the number of organizations encouraging their employees to pursue National Vocational Qualifications (NVQ), those that have purchased interactive video disc systems and organizations such as Motorola that have set up their own universities; the aim of the Motorola University is to improve individual and organizational performance and productivity on a global basis. If due consideration of these needs (i.e. those of the organization as a whole and its individual members of the workforce), is not given, meeting the needs of one may neglect the needs of the other. This not only has repercussions at an organizational level but can also be considered paramount at a national level.

Figure 5.1 depicts a simple training philosophy (McQuater et al., 1995). What the model suggests is that once an organization recognizes a TQM training need, the usual response is to train all members of the workforce regardless of their previous knowledge and skills. The training being carried out is that relating to basic TQM philosophy and how it applies to the organization's strategies, objectives and targets. Carrying on from this initial aware-

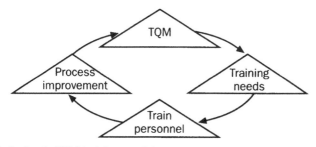

Figure 5.1 A simple TQM training model

ness training, it is then usual to offer education and training in basic tools such as cause and effect analysis, control charts, Pareto analysis, flow charting etc., the key elements of the quality management system and other techniques such as SPC and FMEA. The outcome of the training is that every member of the workforce becomes aware of TQM and should be encouraged and able to apply the philosophies and skills acquired to their own working environment. The cycle is continuous to cover new employees and changing circumstances, to meet customer contractual requirements (current and new), and to facilitate the improvement process. Consequently, processes should be improved, and problems solved permanently, leading to increased efficiency and ultimately providing a more flexible environment to meet the challenges of a global market. However, the theory of this will only become a reality if the education and training given are supported and encouraged by senior management and when what is taught is seen as relevant and can be put into practice. Reality is rarely so clear cut.

In practice, there is little evidence to suggest that organizations give sufficient thought to the training needs of their workforce. There is usually a failure by management to take into consideration the local environment, the intellectual capabilities of their employees, the specific jobs they are carrying out, and the overall workforce skills at their disposal. The use, understanding and application of any given technique or tool is very much dependent on the individual's job. For example, it is more likely that someone in a production/operations position will use control charts, check sheets, and cause and effect analysis than, say, personnel in maintenance, stores or even sales and marketing functions.

In practice, the model outlined in figure 5.1 starts to break down in several ways. During the process of defining organizational training requirements there are several issues to be considered. Training is usually offered to organizations as prepackaged modules and programmes, often resulting from management consultants' and training organizations' prescriptions geared for general application. What this often fails to take into consideration is the individual nature of each organization, their different businesses, processes and products/services, the state of TQM development and maturity, and the issues being faced at the time of the training intervention. All too often, organizations are sold what they requested when something else is what they really needed.

The starting point of defining training needs should be the nature of the business itself. What is right for one organization may not be right for another. Organizations already familiar with techniques such as SPC and FMEA and problem solving methodologies will have a quite different starting point from those introducing improvement concepts for the first time. The difficulty then is structuring the training so that it becomes meaningful to the given audience. Problems start to arise in those companies that have implemented one or more improvement initiatives, which may or may not be compatible with the current initiative, are not integrated and in some cases are in direct conflict with each other. The prevailing attitude then is of 'flavour of the month', with the workforce only paying lip-service to the new initiative.

A potential difficulty facing trainers is that they are asked to provide training on either TQM in general or on a specific facet of the concept, with the course content left to their discretion. This, without any diagnosis of the situation, allows them to choose the material that suits their purposes and that they are comfortable with delivering. This often then becomes a case of the trainer satisfying his or her own needs and, by implication, neglecting the requirements of both the individual and the organization. This, of course, is a generalization and is not true of all trainers. However, following a similar pattern of thought, training managers are often allocated a budget and to make it cost effective the numbers in the training session start to become more important than the appropriateness or timeliness of it – the so-called 'bums on seats' concept. The points being made here lend themselves to a situation recognized by Bramley and Kitson (1994), where trainers use an individual training and education model that places emphasis on encouraging the trainees to learn something thought by the trainer to be useful and then expects them to find practical uses for the training that has been delivered.

In many cases it is often considered a requirement to get all people in the organization trained as quickly as possible (i.e. sheep dipping). The objective behind this is to ensure that people do not feel left out; it reduces resistance to change; a common message is being given; it enhances awareness; and the training will produce a groundswell that will encourage changes in behaviour and attitudes. One of the difficulties presented by this situation is to identify and then provide the best skills and experience mix of trainees during the training sessions. This is crucial in aid-

Workshop Evaluation Form

Workshop date: _____   Location: _____

1 To what extent did the workshop meet your objectives/expectations?

Not at all   Completely

2 Was the objective of the workshop clear to you during the sessions?

No Yes

3 In your opinion did the workshop meet these objectives?

Hardly   Completely

4 Was the attention paid to the different subjects evenly distributed?

No Yes

5 Your opinion of presentations:
   Use of facilities (visuals, flipcharts)
   Presentation techniques in general

Bad   Good

6 What did you think of the venue:
   Refreshments and meals
   Meeting room arrangements

Bad   Good

7 What is your opinion of the time spent on:
   Presentation
   Exercises and evaluation
   Questions

Too little   Too much

8 What did you like most? And why?

9 What did you consider was 'below standard' and should be improved?

10 What should be added to the workshop and what kind of further support do you need?

11 What could be omitted?

12 Are you now going to apply these principals to your project involvement activities?

13 Please add any further comments and suggestions.

Figure 5.2 Training workshop evaluation form   *Source:* Gillifant

ing the learning process. Operators can be intimidated by the presence of supervisors and managers in the training seminars. Conversely, managers and supervisors may feel that their positions are threatened if they openly state their confusion or failure to understand a concept. In both situations trainees will come away from the training dissatisfied and unable to apply what they have been taught.

It is important that training in tools and techniques is not carried out on an ad hoc basis. It ought to be carefully planned and implemented one stage at a time. There is little to be gained by training all people in QFD, for example, when only a small proportion can actually apply it to their own jobs or functions. In a similar vein, training should be timely to coincide with the need, for example, to use and apply a tool or technique, and not when it is convenient for the trainer or even for the organization (i.e. just-in-time training). Training carried out too far in advance of a need is wasteful of resources, since by the time it is used the fundamentals will be forgotten. The training will just have provided the knowledge and understanding; these are not assets unless the skills are developed and this requires patience and practice. In the skill development relating to the use and application of tools and techniques, workplace support and encouragement are essential. If they are lacking, the potential benefits will not be translated into operational improvements, and may even be lost.

Organizations must not become obsessed with the mechanics of training in tools and techniques at the expense of losing sight of the purpose, where the means can undermine the ends. Similarly, they must not detract from value-added education and training as opposed to the amount that is taking place in order to satisfy some directive, company policy, quality award scheme or customer requirement. Employees do not have to become proficient in the more complex techniques if they can understand that there are tools available to aid the problem solving process in their own area of responsibility, since the skills required to apply the more complex techniques can be learnt in time. Under these circumstances, it becomes important to assess both the training event and its outcome. Generally, evaluation of training, using post-course questionnaires, is of the course content, its delivery and the skills and knowledge of the trainer. A typical example of a course evaluation form is given in figure 5.2. The impact in practice of training, particularly its long-term effects and influences, is rarely assessed, even in those organizations that have written procedures to ensure that evaluation is undertaken.

Company-wide training programmes – 'sheep dipping' – may only become effective if the outcome is a sustainable and positive change in organizational behaviour and attitudes towards continuous improvement. However, even this type of training may alienate workers because it does not recognize their needs. The knock-on effect is that it also fails to satisfy the needs of the organization, hindering continuous improvement and sapping valuable resources in the process.

Thus, the dilemma facing the training manager is to identify and determine the organization's education and training requirements as well as those of an individual. For example, the organization as a whole has to be educated in matters relating to increasing quality awareness, with appropriate training that can be presented to suit the person with average educational abilities. However, for individuals who have difficulty with even basic literacy and numeracy and who are required to use basic tools in the processes for which they are the owner, this may be inadequate and something more fundamental may have to be used.

Workforce Skills

Recent studies (e.g. Mason et al., 1994); and Bierhof and Prais, 1993) have shown the existence of differences in the educational levels of workforces throughout Europe, particularly between the UK and Germany (Steedman et al., 1991). This has a direct bearing on the utilization of the workforce skills that are available, since these discrepancies are thought to have a direct effect on productivity and competitiveness in different manufacturing markets. One of the questions is how the differences manifest themselves in the understanding and use of tools and techniques and the TQM training model, shown in figure 5.1.

It has become apparent during the course of the UMIST research that the nature of an employee's job is a major determinant of the actual use of tools and techniques. It is noticeable that use of tools and techniques is on a continuum, they being more likely to be used and applied to processes by those employees with higher skill levels. At the very lowest skills level tools and techniques – which may be an integral part of the job – may be used to a lesser extent because of the lack of perceived benefits. That is, if employees cannot see how a tool or technique is going to help them in their jobs, they tend to pay only lip-service to it. On the other hand, those with higher skills and who are more able to apply critical thought require a sense of purpose for the use of any given technique or tool, needing to see how it can contribute to problem solving. The differences between perceived benefits and a sense of purpose may be somewhat grey, but in sustaining continuous improvement, resolving these types of issues is crucial and will require rationalizing the basic TQM training philosophy. To tackle the issue of changing attitudes to tools and techniques, organizations must examine the profile of their workforce themselves.

Over the past few years problems with numeracy in the UK have become a major concern across all sectors of industry. For example, the first skills audit carried out by the government, and published with the third competitiveness White Paper, pointed out that the UK is 'slipping further behind its rivals in the skills and education of its workforce and shows that the UK workforce has an alarming lack of basic numeracy and literacy skills required to understand simple production information'. Those teaching engineering at university have started to complain about the lack of mathematical ability they are witnessing in their students, and many departments have started to put on additional classes to assist the transition. A recent report by Prais (1993) indicated that a third of all children tested in mathematics were out-scored by the lowest tenth of the same age group of children in Switzerland. Since many continental European countries follow the same basic curriculum it can only be supposed that in the UK it is only those children with exceptional mathematical capabilities who will be able to match the skills of their European counterparts. Therefore, the difficulty facing British industry is first to recognize and diagnose if this is a problem, then to set about educating those who need to attain the desired standard before they are subjected to job- and quality-related skills training.

An example of the difficulties arising from a lack of basic education was clearly identified by observing a small group of shop-floor workers in a UK plant who were undergoing computerized interactive training on SPC, using one of the commonly available video disc training packages. They were required to answer questions on what they had learned at the end of the session. It became apparent that, without the prompting of an SPC facilitator, few of the questions would have been answered correctly.

This may have been due in part to poorly composed questions, raising questions about the suitability of the training package. However, it appeared more likely that the people themselves did not have the educational framework and the training required for it to become an effective training event and tool. The actual utilization of the workforce skills is re-emphasized in this example. SPC facilitators were used to plug the deficit, a situation mirrored frequently throughout British industry. In these circumstances operatives do not even need to understand SPC or its application, because they can rely on others to do it for them. This problem of literacy and numeracy often results in cells or work teams taking responsibility for the interpretation of the data generated by SPC and therefore control of the processes.

At lower to mid-skill levels in organizations understanding of the use of techniques and tools, particularly the more mathematically based ones, varies considerably. Although this may not be solely down to educational differences, this certainly one of the more important factors. In the UK there has been a demise in craft and technician level apprenticeship training where mathematics and communication studies formed an integral part of the course work (Smithers and Robinson, 1991). Since the British education structure appears to discourage students from taking maths, science and engineering subjects in future studies (Wolf, 1993), the shortfall of these capabilities is becoming noticeable at intermediate skill levels. This compares badly with the German dual education system, where even low-ability students undergo vocational training that allows them to transfer their classroom knowledge and understanding to develop their skills in practical situations. This strong grounding in mathematics and engineering enables German organizations to engineer quality into their products using a variety of methods.

The point being made here is that although education and workforce skills are paramount to the use and application of tools and techniques, there are other issues that must be considered. For example, the British organizational culture is to encourage the manager 'who loves a challenge', which engenders firefighting and short-term problem solving. It is this very flexibility that has facilitated the introduction of TQM in many organizations, but the firefighting mentality causes problems with sustaining the initiative and changes in behavioural attitudes. On the other hand, German companies have a very structured culture that actively discourages flexible working, and therefore creates difficulty in developing improvement initiatives, in particular across functional boundaries and at lower levels of the organization. With the introduction· of TQM and the concept of empowerment, fear and suspicion arise because these barriers – some may even say safety nets – are no longer there. Fear and suspicion are not only caused through a lack of education and training but are also in part due to the fundamental human distrust of change. This can result in a lack of cooperation, with only lip-service being paid to any shift in the power base. There is also a tendency in the German plant to revert to the traditional hierarchical method of working when any form of pressure is exerted.

It would be entirely inappropriate to transpose training from the UK to Germany and vice versa. Some aspects would be possible, others not. This affects, in several ways, the TQM training model outlined in figure 5.1. Although the basic model may still be appropriate, it is sub-levels within each category that must be addressed. To facilitate the training under the TQM aspect of the model, organizations should remove themselves from the situation where TQM training is more to satisfy some award criteria or customer requirements than to address the purpose of the concept. When looking at the training needs of all employees involved, issues such as organizational structure, worker profiles, internal and external environments ought to be considered. 'Sheep dipping' does have a place in the model in that all members of the organization must become aware of what TQM is about; however, anything other than awareness programmes ought to be more specifically targeted on a 'need-to-know' basis.

Not all workers need to be trained in every tool and technique, although they all ought to be aware of the existence of the more basic tools. It is far more essential that they receive training in skills necessary to their jobs. In the case of low skilled workers, there may even be scope to introduce related NVQs in mathematics and English; this sort of targeted training will in all probability be more cost effective in the long run. However, caution must be exercised. Booth (1991) has suggested that with the increased reliance on employers to provide training this is more likely to improve the skills of the more educated members of the workforce. Consequently, they are more aware of their shortcomings and more eloquent in stating their needs. Therefore, the skill levels of the general workforce are not enhanced.

Summary

What this chapter has set out to illustrate is that by following the described TQM training model without consideration of other factors, any training carried out will not be effective. The effects and consequences of organizations not taking into consideration the educational standards of their employees or failing in their understanding of workforce skills can be considerable. Although this has particular reference to tools and techniques, it may be allied to a range of organization and individual training events. Awareness training by 'sheep dipping' still has a place, particularly with new employees, but what is advocated here is specific and defined training to raise the workforce skill levels. It must also be stressed that any training that is given, especially in-house, ought to be evaluated and its effectiveness assessed. This too must be part of the continuous improvement process. The expected outcome is an enhancement of the individual's skills profile – and, therefore, that of the organization – by providing the means to achieve competitive goals.

In the UK the effect of the change in post-compulsory education and training over the last generation has had some impact on the use of not just the more mathematically based techniques, but also of the simpler tools requiring basic levels of numeracy and literacy. The implications of this are significant, not least for the multinational organizations that are applying and deploying policies decided at corporate level. They have to consider very carefully the education and training needs of the organization and the individuals in each country. For techniques and tools to be used in an efficient and effective manner, they must be suited to the process and function to which they are being applied.

It is important to identify a standard set of tools and techniques that can be used by everyone, comprising those that are specific to functions and those that are more advanced, the training and expertise being related to this classification. While tools and techniques should never be considered as the domain of the expert, the quality professional enables effective deployment, particularly of those techniques that are more specialized and advanced.

The hierarchy of use and application of tools and techniques has implications for firms that are downsizing and delayering. In some cases such action has removed those people who are more likely to use and apply tools and techniques to their greatest effect. This is not to say that lower levels of the workforce are not able to use them, but their level of understanding is less than that of staff with more technical skills. It may be that those of lesser skills ought to receive the level of training appropriate to their ability levels and competencies. This would not deract from the basic TQM tenet of worker participation in the continuous improvement process, but may actually encourage people to participate, without undermining their ability.

6 An Overview of Common Tools

Introduction

Most organizations use tools and techniques as an aid to improvement. They are commonly used to assist with improvement projects and to solve problems, and are increasingly being used as a routine approach to day-to-day data collection, problem solving and data handling.

There is a vast number of tools and techniques, and this chapter provides an overview of those tools that are in common use by organizations. The examples given of the tools are from organizations with which the authors have carried out work. The aim is to provide a handy reference and a practical guide for all those involved in continuous improvement. The focus is on describing the tools and their uses, along with guidance on construction along the lines of what it is, when to use it, why use it and how to use it. More detailed advice on construction can be found in texts such as Dale (1994), Ishikawa (1976), Juran (1988), Kane (1989), Oakland (1993) and Ozeki and Asaka (1990). For each tool the typical difficulties associated with it are given, along with tips and guidance for overcoming the difficulties.

Activity Sampling

The general purpose of activity sampling is to determine within a specified degree of accuracy the amount of time/frequency spent on specific tasks. This is done through a limited number of discrete observations, rather than having to observe the activity under study on a continuous basis.

The basic steps for designing an activity sampling study are:

- Decide on the activities to be studied.
- Carry out a pilot study to identify the elements of work.
- Plan the survey. This should include briefings of those carrying out the survey, the observations that are to be taken, consulting with everyone concerned in the study, and ensuring that the conditions are as normal as possible.
- Design an observation recording sheet and carry out a preliminary survey to estimate the proportion of time occupied by the activities being measured.
- Determine the number of observations needed to obtain a result of the accuracy desired. For example, with a 95% confidence level $N = [4P (100 - P)]/L^2$, where N is the number of observations needed, P is the percentage of time occupied by the activity and L is the required limit of accuracy
- Carry out the defined number of observations.
- Determine the percentage of time occupied by the activity.
- Calculate the limit of accuracy for this percentage of time using the formula:

$$L = \pm 2 \sqrt{\left[P \frac{(100 - P)}{N} \right]}$$

Difficulties associated with activity sampling are:

- Failing to predetermine all of the variations of different conditions that may affect the work being studied. If the period chosen is not representative then the sample will be biased and the results misleading.
- Making fixed intervals for observations for work that follows a set pattern.
- Failing to make the necessary administrative arrangements, including briefing the operators to ensure that people are aware of the study and its aims. This problem leads to the view that it is another of those 'checking up on what you are doing' exercises and fear that it will lead to job cuts and/or additional work.
- An overly complex observation recording sheet.
- Trying to get an overly accurate result and hence collecting too

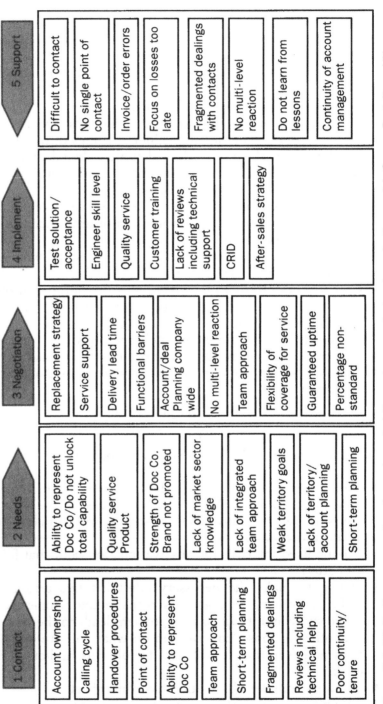

What are the issues involved in losing customers?

1 Contact	2 Needs	3 Negotiation	4 Implement	5 Support
Account ownership	Ability to represent Doc Co/Do not unlock total capability	Replacement strategy	Test solution/acceptance	Difficult to contact
Calling cycle	Quality service Product	Service support	Engineer skill level	No single point of contact
Handover procedures	Strength of Doc Co. Brand not promoted	Delivery lead time	Quality service	Invoice/order errors
Point of contact	Lack of market sector knowledge	Functional barriers	Customer training	Focus on losses too late
Ability to represent Doc Co	Lack of integrated team approach	Account/deal Planning company wide	Lack of reviews including technical support	Fragmented dealings with contacts
Team approach	Weak territory goals	No multi-level reaction	CRID	No multi-level reaction
Short-term planning	Lack of territory/account planning	Team approach	After-sales strategy	Do not learn from lessons
Fragmented dealings	Short-term planning	Flexibility of coverage for service		Continuity of account management
Reviews including technical help		Guaranteed uptime		
Poor continuity/tenure		Percentage non-standard		

Figure 6.1 Affinity diagram: grouping of causals against the customer contact cycle evaluation model. *Source:* Rank Xerox UK

much data, rather than working at a level of accuracy adequate for the study.

Overcome the difficulties by:

• Keeping observations objective.
• Careful briefing of the recorders before the study commences.
• Planning the study so that observations are taken over a representative period.
• Conducting periodic checks during the observation period to ensure that the observers are consistent and accurate and that the observations are being made correctly.
• Ensuring that observations are instantaneous. The recorder must not be influenced by what was taking place immediately before or after the moment of observation.

Finally, when people know that their activities are being studied, they tend to work more conscientiously. To minimize bias due to human reactions, consideration should be given to discarding the initial recordings.

Affinity Diagram

Affinity diagrams are used to categorize verbal data about previously unexplored issues, problems and themes that are hazy, uncertain, complex and difficult to understand, thereby helping to create order out of chaos. They are used in conjunction with or as an alternative to brainstorming, and are useful when new thoughts and ideas are needed. The diagram uses the natural affinity between opinions and partial data from a variety of situations to help understand and structure the problem. It tends to be a creative rather than a logical process. The diagram helps to organize data, ideas, issues and concerns for decision making and to reach solutions about previously unresolved problems. Figure 6.1 shows an example of an affinity diagram from Rank Xerox UK in relation to the customer contact cycle. The customer contact cycle (CCC) is an analysis tool that provides a way of understanding how Rank Xerox supports its customers.

The basic steps for developing an affinity diagram are:

- Decide and clarify the issue, opportunity or theme.
- Collect whatever data is currently available on the theme. This could involve interviews with relevant personnel, customers and suppliers, an examination of notes, complaints and reports, brainstorming, getting people to express opinions etc.
- Each idea, note and need is written on a card or note.
- The cards are placed in a random fashion on the table, board, wall or whatever means is being used to display the data.
- Those cards with related ideas are placed together and separated from the remaining cards. This development of related issues and natural clusters is often done by the team members moving the cards around the board in an atmosphere of silence. The idea of this is to allow the more creative right-hand part of the brain to be used. Team discussion can help to develop the individual statements, ideas etc. on the cards within the cluster. Each group of cards is given a title which reflects the characteristics of the group. The group of stacked cards is then treated as one card. This group card is usually termed the affinity card.
- This process is repeated until all ideas are clustered within different groups.
- The group affinity cards, usually between five and ten, are arranged in a logical order and broad lines are drawn around them.

Difficulties associated with affinity diagrams are:

- Uncertainty about when to use them and their benefits in comparison to other tools such as brainstorming and relationship diagrams.
- The tendency to put more than one idea on a card.
- Lack of group participation.
- Failure to work as a team.
- Data presented in an unmanageable form.
- Traditional thinking based on previous experiences.

Overcome the difficulties by:

- Ensuring that all relevant data on the theme has been identified and is available.
- Keeping a relaxed and creative atmosphere when developing the diagram.
- Grouping the ideas in silence to prevent traditional arguments surfacing.

- Encouraging breakthrough thinking.
- Allowing relationship of ideas to develop in a natural manner.
- Not being be afraid to allow ideas to stand alone.
- Spending time working out an appropriate title for the affinity card.
- Using the output as the platform for further action.

Arrow Diagram

This method applies systematic thinking to the planning and execution of a complex set of tasks. It is used to establish the most suitable plan for a series of activities in a project, and to monitor its progress in an efficient manner to ensure adherence to the schedule. Arrow diagrams are necessary to describe the interrelationships and dependencies of tasks within a complex job or project. They are deployed at the implementation planning stage of a project, which is always the critical stage. The sequence of the steps involved and their relation to each other are indicted by arrows and in this way a network of activities is developed. This method, its form of construction, and the calculation and identification of critical paths are well known. The technique is used in project management in relation to critical path analysis (CPA) and the programme evaluation and review technique (PERT). Figure 6.2 is an example of an arrow diagram constructed by the part-time improvement facilitators at Betz Dearborn in relation to the siting and construction of a quality notice board.

The key steps in constructing an arrow diagram are:

- Identify all activities needed to complete the plan.
- Decide the feasible sequence of the activities:
  - which activities must precede certain activities (consecutive activities)
  - which activities must follow an activity (consecutive activities)
  - which activities can be done at the same time (concurrent or parallel activities)
- Arrange the diagram from left to right according to the above logic with each activity represented by an arrow.
- The beginning or end of an activity or group of activities is called an event or node, and these are represented as circles at

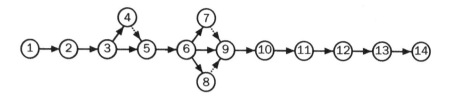

Notes

Activities

1–2   Choose locations
2–3   Assign responsibilities
3–4   Determine size and configuration of displays needed
3–5   Consider health and safety implications of potential locations
5–6   Establish public relations departments' stock of displays and their availability
6–7   Determine method of display (free-standing/wall-mounted)
6–8   Determined preferred 'editorial content' of displays
6–9   Action update of display contents
7–9   Obtain costings for additional/alternative displays
9–10   Source initial display items (e.g. graphs, photographs, successes)
10–11   Agree format and action the 'design a logo' competition
11–12   Arrange for displays to be sited/mounted
12–13   Review cost implications
13–14   Seek verbal feedback from site employees

Figure 6.2 Arrow diagram: siting of a quality notice board. *Source*: Betz Dearborn

the tail and head of an arrow. The events should be numbered in the order in which activities occur.
- The time required for each activity is indicated under the appropriate arrow.
- Analyse the network to find the critical path and to establish in which activities there is free time (float). This is achieved by determining the earliest and latest event times.

Difficulties associated with arrow diagrams are:

- Lack of understanding of the project activities and implementation objectives.
- Deciding the feasible sequence of the project activities that have been identified.
- Establishing the dependencies of activities.

- Calculation of float (i.e. the amount of time by which an activity can extend beyond its duration without affecting the overall time for the project).
- Incorrect use of dummy activities (these are used to preserve the unique numbering system and the network logic).

Overcome the difficulties by:

- Double-checking the dependencies/relationships between activities and tasks.
- Exercising judgement as to the level of detail needed.
- Ensuring that time estimates are as accurate as possible.
- Using computer-based packages for more complex projects.

Brainstorming

Brainstorming is a method of free expression and is employed when the solutions to problems cannot be deduced logically and/or when creative new ideas are required. It is used with a wide variety of tools and techniques. Brainstorming works best in groups. It unlocks the creative power of the group through the synergistic effect (e.g. one person's ideas may trigger the thoughts of another member of the group) and in this way stimulates the production of ideas. The aim is to generate the greatest possible number of ideas in a short space of time. It can be employed in a structured manner, in which the group follows a set of rules, or in an unstructured format, which allows anyone in the group to present ideas randomly as they occur.

The following are some factors to be considered when organizing a brainstorming session:

- Prepare a clear and focused statement of the problem.
- Form a group and appoint a leader/facilitator. A team will always produce a greater number of ideas than the same number of individuals working in isolation.
- Elect someone to record the ideas as precisely and explicitly as possible, ideally on a flipchart to maintain a visible and permanent record or on a whiteboard.
- Review the rules of brainstorming (i.e. code of conduct); for example:

- each member in rotation is asked for ideas
- a member can only offer one idea in turn
- the ideas are stated in as few words as possible
- where a member has no ideas he or she simply says 'pass'
- strive for an explosion of ideas and build on the ideas of other group members
- accept all ideas as given and record them; questions are only asked to clarify issues
- no criticism, discussion, interruptions, comments or judgements are made during brainstorming
- ideas are not evaluated during the brainstorming session
- good-natured laughter and informality enhance the environment for innovative activity
- exaggeration adds humour and often provides a creative stimulus

- Review the typical difficulties encountered in brainstorming, in order to prevent or minimize their occurrence.
- Determine the best ideas by consensus. This can be done in a number of ways – majority voting or polling, Pareto voting, paired comparisons, ranking on a scale (e.g. 1–10), or each team member ranks the items in order of priority with 5 points given to the first idea and 3 and 1 points given respectively to the second and third ideas etc.
- As ideas are suggested these are written down in such a way that they can be seen by all members of the group.
- Allow the ideas to incubate for a period of time before they are evaluated.

Difficulties associated with brainstorming are:

- Quality of output is not as good as expected.
- Criticisms of individuals and lack of cohesion among group members.
- Inappropriate balance of people in the session.
- Side discussions and members trying to talk all together.
- A person attempting to play the role of an 'expert'.
- Poor management of the process (e.g. leader dominates the group).
- Members shouting out ideas when it is not their turn.
- Sessions being too long.
- Size of the group being too small or too large.
- Attempting to evaluate ideas during brainstorming.

- A tendency to state 'solutions' rather than possible causes.
- Omission of ideas, by the person responsible for writing down the ideas suppressing those that he or she does not agree with (the power of the pen).
- Failure to use flipcharts, whiteboards etc. to visually display the data.

Overcome the difficulties by:

- Ensuring that the topic to be 'brainstormed' is well defined and understood by all those involved.
- Ensuring that the right people are involved.
- Creating a relaxed and comfortable environment.
- Considering a 'warm-up' session relating to a simple problem.
- Evaluating the output against the topic to be brainstormed.
- Developing a classification to represent the degree to which events can be controlled, (e.g. Total (T), Partial (P) and Not (N)).
- Sticking to the rules of brainstorming, especially not evaluating ideas as they are suggested.
- Ensuring that listings of ideas are clear.
- Allowing the ideas to incubate before they are evaluated.
- Keeping the participants focused on the topic.
- Avoiding interruption and distraction.
- Determining the best ideas by consensus.
- Delegating recording and leading of the process to team members to promote their involvement, participation and ownership.
- Ensuring that the 'scribe' records all ideas and ensuring that the pace of the session is controlled to facilitate this.
- If ideas dry up, allowing any person to contribute ideas in a random manner.

Cause and Effect Diagram

This type of diagram was developed by the late Kaoru Ishikawa to determine and break-down the main causes of a given problem. Cause and effect diagrams are often called Ishikawa diagrams or 'fishbone' diagrams because of their skeletal appearance. They are usually employed where there is only one problem and its possible causes are hierarchical in nature.

The effect (a specific problem or a quality characteristic/condition) is considered to be the head, and potential causes and sub-causes of the problem, or quality characteristics/conditions, to be the bone structure of the fish. The diagrams illustrate in a clear manner the possible relationships between some identified effect and the causes influencing it. They also assist in helping to uncover the root causes of a problem and in generating improvement ideas.

They are typically used by a quality control circle, quality improvement team, Kaizen team, problem solving team etc., as part of a brainstorming exercise to solicit ideas and opinions as to the possible major cause(s) of the problem, and subsequently to offer recommendations to resolve or counteract the problem.

It is important to define the problem or abnormality clearly, giving as much detail as possible, to enable the identification of potential causes. This can be quite a difficult task, and the team leader must assume responsibility for defining a manageable problem (if it is too large it may need to be subdivided into a number of sub-problems) to ensure that the team's efforts and contributions are maximized in a constructive manner. There are three types of diagrams:

1 *5M cause and effect diagram.* The main 'bone' structure or branches typically comprise Machinery, Manpower, Method, Material and Maintenance. Often teams omit maintenance, and hence use a 4M diagram, while others may add a sixth 'M' (Mother Nature) and so use a 6M diagram. The 4M, 5M or 6M diagram is useful for those with little experience of constructing cause and effect diagrams and is a good starting point in the event of any uncertainty. In non-manufacturing areas the 4Ps (Policies, Procedures, People and Plant) are sometimes found to be more appropriate. As with any type of cause and effect diagram, the exact format is not so important as the process of bringing about appropriate countermeasures for the identified and agreed major cause(s) for the problem.

2 *Process cause and effect diagram.* This is usually used when the problem encountered cannot be isolated to a single section or department. The team members should be familiar with the process under consideration, therefore it is usual to map it out using a flow chart and seek to identify potential causes for the problem at each stage of the process. If the process flow is so large as to be unmanageable, the sub-processes or process steps

should be identified separately. Each stage of the process is then brainstormed and ideas developed using, for example a 4M, 5M or 6M format. The key causes are identified for further analysis.
3 *Dispersion analysis cause and effect diagram.* This diagram is usually used after a 4M, 5M or 6M diagram has been completed. The major causes identified by the group are then treated as separate branches and expanded upon by the team.

Figure 6.3 shows an example of a cause and effect diagram from Cerestar UK Ltd with respect to a project to improve the efficiency of the production of dextrose.

Cause and effect diagrams are usually produced via a team approach and involve the following basic steps:

- Ensure that every team member understands the problem and develop a clear problem statement.
- Define with clarity; write in a box to the right the key symptom or effect of the problem and draw a horizontal line from the left of the box.
- Decide the major groupings or categories for the causes of the effect, these form the main branches of the diagram.
- In a brainstorming session, the group members speculate on causes of the effect; and these are added to the branches or sub-branches of the diagram.
- In a subsequent session the causes are discussed and analysed to determine those that are most likely to have caused the effect.
- The most likely or major causes of the problem are ranked, by the group, in order of importance. This can be done by Pareto voting; 80 per cent of the votes should be cast for 20 per cent of the causes. (If, for example, there are thirty-five causes, using the figure of 20 per cent gives each member seven votes to allocate to what they believe are the causes of the effect).
- Additional data is sometimes gathered to confirm the key causes.

Difficulties associated with cause and effect diagrams and analysis are:

- Poorly defined and understood effect.
- Deciding the titles of the main groupings.

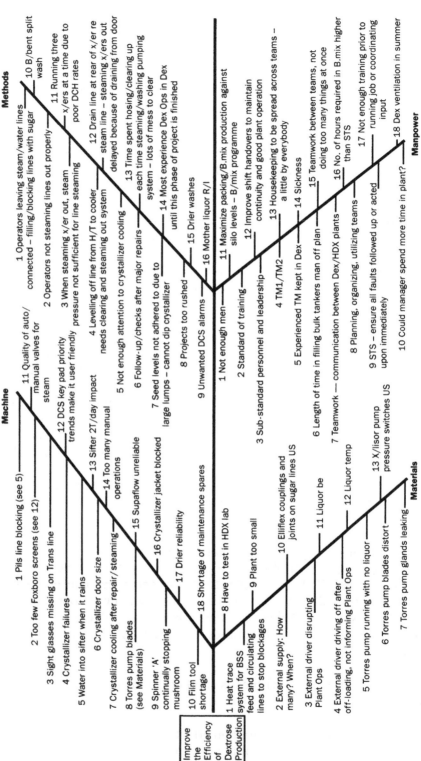

Figure 6.3 Cause and effect diagram: efficiency of dextrose production. *Source:* Cerestar UK

- Tackling too large an issue.
- Perceived as 'glorified brainstorming and an unnecessary formality'.
- Constructing the diagram can be perceived as time consuming.
- Deciding to which arm of the diagram an idea is to be allocated.
- Failure to build on the causes of the effect that have already been identified.
- Naming/blaming individuals (i.e. not wishing to identify causes of the effect to the manpower branch of the diagram).
- Not using brainstorming techniques.
- Used by an individual and not by a team, consequently important causes of the effect are not identified.
- Selecting the root cause from all of the ideas presented.
- Mixing symptoms with causes.
- Persuading people outside the group that constructed the diagram to use it to take action.

Overcome the difficulties by:

- Ensuring that the team is focused on the effect.
- If an issue becomes unmanageable due to its scope and complexity, encouraging further subdivisions of the problem to maximize the team's contribution (i.e. a dispersion analysis cause and effect diagram).
- Deciding which cause goes under which category should not be subject to discussion at the time of developing ideas; the important factor is the idea. It should not be forgotten that the convention only suggests a starting point. This should not be allowed to become an issue for the team; the analysis can be tidied up later.
- Using words to describe the main categories or branches of the diagram that are recognized and understood throughout the organization, such as environment, health and safety etc.
- Naming and in extreme cases blaming individuals can lead to mistrust and must be avoided. It is more acceptable to list a function, e.g. Purchasing or Accounts. Problem solving or getting to the root causes of a problem is usually associated with the 'management system' or process and should be treated as such.
- Having identified many possible causes of a problem, it may be difficult to decide which ones to focus on. The instinct of the team will provide the best way forward. However, there are

Standard Operating Procedure (SOP): Control Information

Does the SOP clearly state/include the following or make cross-reference to supporting information?

Job title and purpose (why)	Yes	No	
SOP reference number	Yes	No	
Scope of the job covered by the SOP	Yes	No	
Name of person responsible for construction of SOP	Yes	No	
Approval by controlling function	Yes	No	N/A
Last revision date	Yes	No	
Next revision date	Yes	No	
Acceptance by user(s), user friendly	Yes	No	
Reference to supporting information (can the user locate the information using the SOP?)	Yes	No	N/A
Training and refresher training (why?)	Yes	No	N/A
Information on one sheet	Yes	No	
Visual communication to replace words	Yes	No	

Job process information

Does the SOP clearly state/include the following or make cross-reference to supporting information?

Correct (standard) sequence of operations/actions	Yes	No	N/A
Agreed critical control/check points	Yes	No	
Correct job performance by: (1) experienced operator	Yes	No	N/A
(2) inexperienced operator	Yes	No	N/A
Key job requirements (Q,D,C and P)(i.e. quality, cost, delivery and performance)	Yes	No	N/A
Sampling and/or inspection procedures	Yes	No	N/A
Actions and limits of authority in dealing with abnormalities	Yes	No	N/A
Fault finding actions	Yes	No	N/A
Supplier/customer (next operation/action)	Yes	No	N/A
Technical specifications	Yes	No	N/A

Q,D,C,P (S&M) Information

Does the SOP clearly state/include the following or make cross-reference to supporting information?

Possible (most common) abnormalities	Yes	No	
Methods of monitoring and recording abnormalities	Yes	No	N/A
Reference and requirements of any inspection equipment	Yes	No	N/A
Calibration/equipment checking requirements	Yes	No	N/A
Product protection and/or handling requirements (why?)	Yes	No	N/A
Process (operation, lead, queue) times	Yes	No	N/A
Delivery dates (outputs from job)	Yes	No	N/A
High cost items/features (why?)	Yes	No	N/A
Opportunities for job holder cost control	Yes	No	N/A
Potential hazards, warnings (why?)	Yes	No	
Actions in the event of a health and safety problem	Yes	No	
Skill and knowledge requirements (to do the job)	Yes	No	N/A
Location of help and assistance	Yes	No	N/A

Additional SOP information (job-related)

Does the SOP clearly state/include the following information or make cross-reference to supporting information?

Special fail safe devices and purpose (why?)	Yes	No	N/A
Certificates/permits to operate (why?)	Yes	No	N/A
Pre-kitting checks	Yes	No	N/A

Figure 6.4 Inspection and validation checklist covering the construction of standard operating procedures. *Source:* RHP Bearings

other tools and techniques commonly used in these circumstances, including ranking and rating, paired comparisons (for decision making), check sheets and concentration diagrams (for data collection).

● Never losing sight of the fact that problems may rise to the surface where they were not originally caused, so missing the target is quite a possibility.

Checklist

Checklists (sometimes called inspection or validation checklists) are used as prompts and aids to personnel, in particular in terms of facilitating reasoned thinking. They highlight the key features of a process, equipment, system and/or product or service to which attention needs to be given, and ensure that the procedures for an operation, housekeeping, inspection, maintenance etc. have been followed. Checklists are also used in audits of both product and systems. They are an invaluable aid for quality assurance and, as might be imagined, the variety, style and content of such lists are immense. Figure 6.4 is an example of an inspection and validation checklist from RHP Bearings, Newark, covering the construction of standard operating procedures.

The basic steps in constructing a checklist are:

● Study the activity for which the checklist is to be drawn up.
● Drawing on observations of the process, discussions with operatives and appropriate working instructions and procedures, construct the checklist.
● Walk the checklist through the process, by actually following what happens at each stage.
● Ask the operator to check its accuracy.
● Display it next to the process.
● Assess its use in practice.

Difficulties associated with checklists are:

● Overcomplicating them.
● The steps in the list do not reflect the actual situation.
● It is perceived by operatives as having little value.
● Poor clarity of presentation.
● Overconfidence and complacency in their use.

Overcome the difficulties by:

- Defining the process and its boundaries.
- Ensuring that those who are involved in the process have an input into the development of the checklist.
- Carrying out audits at regular intervals to check the validity of the checklist and to assess whether it is being followed.

Check Sheet

A check sheet is a sheet or form used to record data. The check sheet is a simple and convenient recording method for collecting and determining the occurrence of events, including their presentation. The events relate to non-conformities, including the position where they appear on the non-conforming item (when used in this way they are sometimes referred to as 'measles' charts, defect position or concentration diagrams, or areas for concern charts), non-conforming items, breakdowns of machinery and/or associated equipment, non-value-adding activity or, indeed, anything untoward that may occur within a process. Check sheets are helpful in following the maxim of 'no checking or measurement without recording the data'.

They are prepared, in advance of the recording of data, by the operatives and staff being affected by a problem. Check sheets, in table or diagram format, are extremely useful as a data collection device and a record to supplement attribute control charts (see chapter 7). The data from a check sheet provides the factual basis for subsequent analysis and corrective action. There are many different kinds of check sheets. Figure 6.5 is an example of a check sheet from Rexam Corrugated North East Ltd to record the defects encountered in the gluing/stitching department.

The following are the main steps in constructing a check sheet:

- Determine the type of check sheet to use (e.g. tabular form or defect position chart).
- Decide the type of data to be illustrated. The data can relate to: number of defectives, percentage of total defectives, cost of defectives, type of defective, process, equipment, shift, business unit, operator etc.
- Decide which features/characteristics and items are to be checked.

Check item	Week no. Day 1	2	3	4	5	6	7
Warp board							
Board delamination							
Surface defect							
Incorrect board spec.							
Incorrect print density							
Shouldering							
Incorrect ink weight							
Off square feeding							
Print mis-registration							
Split bends							
Deep slots							
Narrow slots							
Ink smudging							

Figure 6.5 Check sheet: gluing/stitching department. *Source*: Rexam Corrugated North East Ltd

- Design the sheet. Ideally, it should be flexible enough to allow the data to be arranged in a variety of ways. Data should always be arranged in the most meaningful way to make best use of it.
- Decide the time period over which data is to be collected.
- Specify the format, instructions and sampling method for recording the data, including the use of appropriate symbols.

Difficulties associated with check sheets are:

- They are not designed by the people who collect or use the data.
- Leaving the sheet with individuals and/or a process for too long before the data is reviewed.

- Not being clear about what data (i.e. checking characteristics) needs to be collected, by both team members and others who are involved in the collection of data.
- Attempting to display too much information on the sheet.
- Concerns about how the data will be used.
- Failure to clearly specify the format, instructions and sampling methods for collecting and recording the data.
- Ensuring that everything is written down.
- The lack of vision to convert, in the future, the check sheet into a multiple characteristic chart.
- Concerns about the time taken to collect and record the data.

Overcome the difficulties by:

- Having a clear purpose for using the check sheet and communicating this to relevant people.
- Involving those who will be collecting the data in the process of designing the check sheet, in particular the features/characteristics to be checked.
- Inviting some of those collecting data to be involved in its subsequent analysis and use.
- Considering making the completion of the check sheet anonymous to avoid the fear factor.
- Regularly reviewing (i.e. weekly) how data collection is progressing.
- Identifying the data needed after the likely root causes have been agreed.
- Ensuring that the collected data is providing the information required by regular review and analysis.
- From the review and analysis modifying, if appropriate, the check sheet, including the rank position of the non-conformities.

Flow Charts

Process mapping (sometimes called 'blueprinting' or process modelling), in either a structured or unstructured format, is a prerequisite to obtaining an in-depth understanding of a process, before the application of techniques such as FMEA, SPC and quality costing. A flow chart is employed to provide a diagrammatic picture, by means of a set of symbols, showing all of the steps or stages in a process, project or sequence of events. It is of considerable assistance in documenting and describing a process as an aid to its subsequent examination and improvement.

A chart, when used in a manufacturing context, may show the complete process from goods-receiving through storage, manufacture and assembly to despatch of final product, or may simply show some part of this process in detail. What is important is that each 'activity' is included to focus attention on aspects of the process or subset of the process where problems have occurred or may occur, to enable some corrective action to be taken or countermeasure to be put in place.

Traditionally, charts (called process charts) have employed conventional symbols to define activities such as operation, inspection, delay or temporary storage, permanent storage and transportation, and are much used by operations and methods and industrial engineering personnel (see Currie (1989) for details). In more recent times they have witnessed considerable use by those involved in business process reengineering (BPR).

There are a number of variants of the classical process flow chart, including those tailored to an individual company's use, with different symbols being used to reflect the situation under study. What is important is not the format of the chart and/or flow diagram, but that the process has been mapped out with key inputs, value-adding steps and outputs defined and is understood by those directly involved and responsible for initiating improvements. Analysing the data collected on a flow chart can help to uncover irregularities and potential problem points. It is also a useful method of dealing with customer complaints, by establishing the cause of the break or problem in the customer–supplier chain and rectifying it by means of corrective action. In a number of cases, processes are poorly defined and documented. Also, in some organizations people are only aware of their own particular aspect of a process, and process mapping helps to facilitate a greater understanding of the whole process. It is essential to the development of the internal customer–supplier relationship. Figures 6.6 is an example of flow charting from British Aerospace Defence Dynamics used on the Rapier GE environmental stress screening process.

The following are the main steps in constructing a flow chart:

• Define the process and its boundaries, including start and end points.

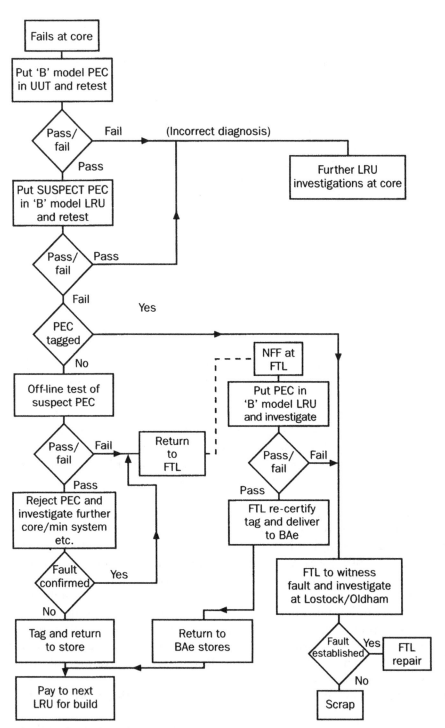

Figure 6.6 Flow chart: Ferranti PECs – core failures. *Source*: British Aerospace Defence Dynamics

- Decide the type and method of charting and the symbols to be used, and do not deviate from the convention chosen.
- Decide the detail with which the process is to be mapped.
- Describe the stages, in sequence, in the process using the agreed methodology.
- Assess whether these stages are in the correct sequence.
- Ask people involved with the process to check its accuracy.

Difficulties associated with flow charts are:

- They can become too complicated.
- The steps indicated on the chart do not reflect the real situation.
- Different people have different views of what the process, project or event entails.
- Use of inappropriate and mismatched symbols and lack of consistency in their application.
- A fear of 'why are you investigating my job?'

Overcome the difficulties by:

- Communicating to all concerned, before the investigation begins, what is intended, why it is being done and what will be done with the resulting information.
- Defining the process and its boundaries.
- Keeping the flow chart simple.
- Avoiding the use of complex symbols.
- Being consistent with the use of symbols.
- Ensuring that those involved in the process are involved with the charting procedure.
- Flow charting the ideal situation and comparing this with the current situation. For more complex processes, supplement the flow charts by 'walking through the process'. This involves actually following what happens at each stage, rather than trying to chart the process from a theoretical or 'would like it to be' base.
- Developing an open and honest environment.

Force Field Analysis

This tool is based on the concept that any problem is a result of forces acting on it. The negative or restraining forces keep the

Diagram constructed by RHP Newark users after six months application of time management principles using the time system tool.

Driving forces	Restricting forces
The additional benefits experienced from the application of effective time management through the time system approach.	The additional requirements and/or disadvantages of using effective time management techniques and the time system tool.

Driving forces

- Nothing is lost or forgotten (reducing stress)
- Database is a portable file (giving more control)
- Teamworking improved (especially with users)
- System allows you to clear your mind (providing more creative space)
- Ability to link activities with goals (doing the right things)
- Ability to set dates and deadlines (more proactive approach)
- Effective prioritizing (doing the right things)
- More can be achieved (right things and smarter)
- Using productive time (prime time activities)
- Reacting effectively to change (coping with unexpected)
- System can be customized (system is for *you*)
- Database of key goals and targets (effective focus and review)
- System produces surprises (seeing what's coming)
- Merging work and home life (System covers and links both)

Restricting forces

- Planning time and discipline needed (change feels uncomfortable)
- Non-users (people not buying-into process)
- Priorities planned by others (especially in low prime time)
- Majority of paperwork in A4 (requires reducing to A5)
- Expectations of others (time system is a tool)
- Cost (initial outlay–investment)
- Blaming the system when failure occurs (not how the system was used)

Figure 6.7 Force field diagram: time management. *Source*: RHP Bearings

problem at its current level while the positive or driving forces push the situation toward improvement. The former are the causes of the problem, the latter are potential solutions. This tool is very often used to identify forces during the process of change. Figure 6.7 shows a force field analysis diagram from RHP Bearings Ltd in relation to the use of time management.

The following are the main steps in constructing a force field diagram:

- Describe the problem.
- If the current level of the problem is too high (e.g. rework) the restraining forces will be in a vertical upward position. If the level of the problem is too low (e.g. communication) the restraining forces will be in a vertical downward position.
- The restraining forces that keep the problem at its current level are first identified. The forces are summarized and connected as a vector to the problem.
- Once a significant number of restraining forces have been identified, improving or driving forces are pinpointed to counteract each specific restraining force.
- The completed diagram presents a specific problem together with potential solutions.

Difficulties associated with force field analysis are:

- Lack of understanding of the tool.
- Inappropriate application.
- Many organizations often forget what they do well, and instead concentrate on their failures.
- Failure to identify appropriate forces.
- Using it as a blame exercise.

Overcome the difficulties by:

- Identifying and focusing on the positive forces before listing the negative ones.
- Ensuring that the most appropriate personnel are involved during the development of the diagram.
- Developing the negative forces in group session then posting in a prominent position the partly completed analysis in the section for employees to add positive forces as and when they like.
- Using the results.

Graphs

Graphs, be they presentational (i.e. to convey data in some pictorial manner) or mathematical (i.e. from which data may be interpolated or extrapolated), are used to facilitate understanding and analysis of the collected data, investigate relationships between factors, attract attention, indicate trends and make the data memorable. Scatter diagrams can be considered as a special form of graph. They are used when examining the possible relationship or association between two variables, characteristics or factors. They indicate the relationship as a pattern – cause and effect. For example, one variable may be a process parameter (e.g. temperature, pressure, screw speed) and the other may be some measurable characteristic or feature of the product (e.g. length, weight, thickness). As the process parameter is changed (independent variable), it is noted together with any measured change in the product variable (dependent variable), and this is repeated until sufficient data have been collected.

There is a wide choice of graphical methods available (line graphs, bar charts, pie charts, Gantt charts, radar charts, band charts) for different types of application. Figure 6.8 gives two examples of graphs from Cerestar UK in relation to customer complaints.

The following are the type of issues that need to be considered in the construction of graphs:

- Use clear titles and indicate when and how the data was collected (i.e. the theme and the source of data).
- Ensure that the scales are clear, understandable and represent the data accurately.
- When possible, use symbols for extra data.
- Always keep in mind the reason why a graph is being used (i.e. to highlight some information or data in a striking and unambiguous way). Anything that facilitates this objective is desirable.

Difficulties associated with graphs are:

- Unrepresentative units of measurement.
- Recording and displaying what can easily be measured rather than what needs to be measured.
- Unrealistic time period over which the data was charted.

- Confounding dependent and independent variables.
- Choice of scales for y and x axis.
- The data presented does not represent a pattern.

Overcome the difficulties by:

- Selecting and defining the data to be charted.
- Using symbols to highlight key points.
- Checking that the data has some form of relationship.
- Interpreting the data and using the results.

Histograms

A histogram is a graphical representation of individual measured values in a data set according to the frequency or relative frequency of occurrence. They take measured data from the tally sheet and display its distribution using the class intervals or value as a base – it resembles a bar chart with the bars representing the frequency of data. The histogram helps to visualise the distribution of data and in this way they reveal the amount of variation within a process. There are several forms which should be recognized – normal, skewed, bimodal, isolated island, etc. There are a number of theoretical models which provide patterns and working tools for various shapes of distribution, the shape of distribution most often encountered is called normal or Gaussian.

There are several ways of constructing histograms depending upon whether the data are discrete or continuous, whether they are single or grouped values and whether there is a vast amount of data or not. The following guidelines are given for the treatment of continuous data of sufficient quantity that grouping is required:

- Subtract the smallest individual value from the largest.
- Divide this range by eight or nine to give the number of classes or groups.
- The resultant value indicates the width or interval of the group. This should be rounded for convenience, e.g. 4.3 could be regarded as either 4 or 5 depending upon the data collected.
- These calculations are undertaken to give approximately eight or nine group class intervals of a rational width.
- Each individual measurement now goes into its respective group or class.

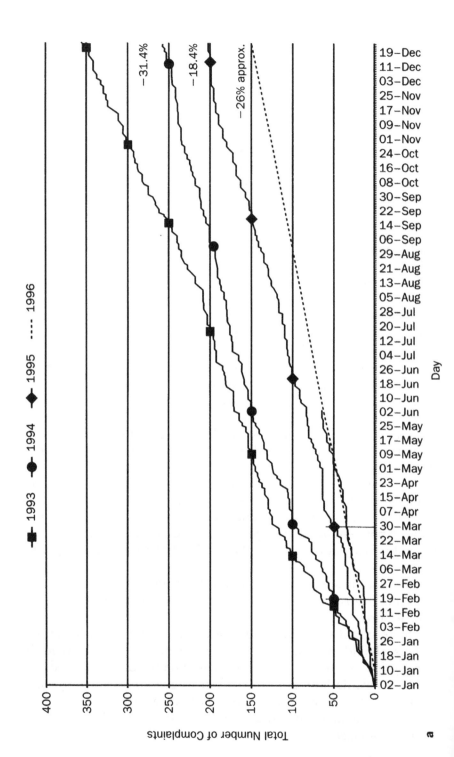

-31.4%

-18.4%

-26% approx.

Day

Total Number of Complaints

—■— 1993   —●— 1994   —◆— 1995   ---- 1996

400 350 300 250 200 150 100 50 0

19-Dec
11-Dec
03-Dec
25-Nov
17-Nov
09-Nov
01-Nov
24-Oct
16-Oct
08-Oct
30-Sep
22-Sep
14-Sep
06-Sep
29-Aug
21-Aug
13-Aug
05-Aug
28-Jul
20-Jul
12-Jul
04-Jul
26-Jun
18-Jun
10-Jun
02-Jun
25-May
17-May
09-May
01-May
23-Apr
15-Apr
07-Apr
30-Mar
22-Mar
14-Mar
06-Mar
27-Feb
19-Feb
11-Feb
03-Feb
26-Jan
18-Jan
10-Jan
02-Jan

a

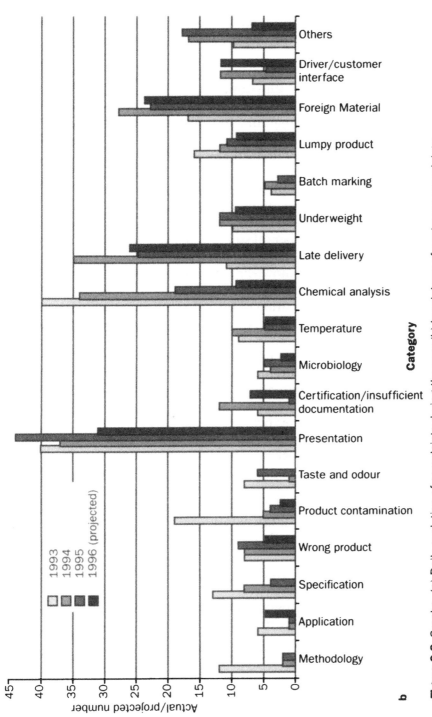

Figure 6.8 Graphs. (a) Daily evolution of complaints during the year (b) breakdown of customer complaints.
Source: Cerestar UK Ltd

- Construct the histogram with measurements on the horizontal scale and frequency (or number of measurements) on the vertical scale.
- The 'blocks' of the histogram should adjoin each other, i.e. there should be no gaps unless there is a recorded zero frequency.
- Clearly label the histogram and state the source of the data.

Difficulties associated with histograms are:

- Lack of awareness of the common forms.
- Inappropriate construction of histogram.
- Failure to collect the data to a predetermined tally sheet.
- Inappropriate number of sub-groups and breakpoints of the data classes.
- Lack of statistical knowledge, which is required for the interpretation of data.
- Inappropriate application of histograms to a particular data set.
- Confusion over what constitutes a histogram and what is a bar chart.
- Ill-defined purpose for using histograms.
- Inappropriate measurements used.
- Confounding the mutually exclusive rule.

Overcome the difficulties by:

- Defining why a histogram is being used.
- Selecting measurements appropriate to the process under investigation.
- Collecting sufficient data to accurately represent the process, usually a minimum of fifty points.
- Using appropriate methods for determining class intervals and class widths.
- Checking all calculations.
- Labelling all axes clearly.
- Interpreting the histogram, and discussing the results and findings with those people involved in the study.

Matrix Diagram

Matrix diagrams are used to clarify the relationship and key connecting points between results and causes or between objectives and methods and to indicate their relative importance. They are also useful for drawing conclusions between consequences and their causes. They are used when there are two sets of factors and methods, which may have no relationship with each other. The factors are arranged in rows and columns on a chart with the intersections identifying the problem and its concentration; the intersecting points are the base for future action and problem solving. Showing, in graphical manner, the complete problem or picture, its essential characteristics and the actions that may impact on the problem is of considerable help in developing a strategy for its resolution. Symbols are used to depict the presence and strength of a relationship between sets of data. There are a number of types of matrix diagrams (e.g. L-type, T-type, Y-type), each having a specific range of applications. Figure 6.9 shows the structure of an L-type matrix used on a Rank Xerox customer retention project.

The major steps in constructing a matrix diagram are:

- Decide the format of the matrix – L-type, T-type, C-type, X-type, etc. – and the characteristics, tasks, problems, causes, methods, measures etc. to be compared, mapped and displayed.
- Decide how to arrange the problems and their causes. For example, in an L-shaped matrix for relating customer needs and design features, the customer needs are listed in the rows and the design features relating to each need are listed in the columns.
- Define and specify the symbols that are to be used to summarize a relationship.
- The relationships between, say, the needs and features or problems and causes etc. are identified and discussed and symbols used to indicate the strength of the relationship where a column and a row intersect.
- Review the completed diagram for accuracy.

Difficulties associated with the matrix diagram:

- Arranging the problems and their causes into rows and columns.

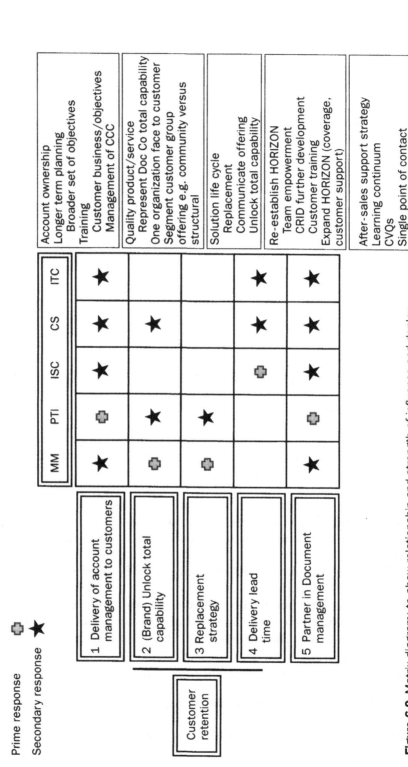

Prime response ✚
Secondary response ★

Customer retention

	MM	PTI	ISC	CS	ITC
1 Delivery of account management to customers	★	✚	★	★	★	Account ownership · Longer term planning · Broader set of objectives · Training · Customer business/objectives · Management of CCC
2 (Brand) Unlock total capability	✚	★	★	★		Quality product/service · Represent Doc Co total capability · One organization face to customer · Segment customer group offering e.g. community versus structural
3 Replacement strategy	✚	★		★		Solution life cycle · Replacement · Communicate offering · Unlock total capability
4 Delivery lead time		✚	✚	★	★	Re-establish HORIZON · Team empowerment · CRID further development · Customer training · Expand HORIZON (coverage, customer support)
5 Partner in Document management	★	✚	★	★	★	After-sales support strategy · Learning continuum · CVQs · Single point of contact · Review, including technical help

Figure 6.9 Matrix diagram: to show relationship and strength of influence and deploy definable and assignable tasks to the organization. *Source: Rank Xerox UK*

- Attempting to force a particular pattern from a set of data.
- Agreeing the degree of correlation/impact of the factors at each intercept.
- Failing to use the data to draw conclusions about priorities.

Overcome the difficulties by:

- Being able to express the subject matter properly in the matrix.
- Basing the choice of matrix format just on the number of items and comparisons that are to be attempted.
- Reaching consensus on the degree of correlation.
- Revisiting the matrix to test if the factors/correlations have changed.

Pareto Analysis

Pareto analysis is a technique employed for prioritizing problems of any type (e.g. quality, production, stock control, sickness, absenteeism, accident occurrences, resource allocation). The analysis highlights the fact that most problems come from a few of the causes and indicates what problems to solve and in what order (e.g. Juran's (1988) 'vital few and trivial many'). In this way the improvement efforts are directed at areas and projects that will have the greatest impact. Pareto analysis is an extremely useful tool for condensing a large volume of data into a manageable form and helping to determine which problems to solve and in what order. A Pareto diagram can be considered as a special form of bar chart.

The analysis was labelled 'Pareto' after the Italian economist Vilfredo Pareto, who observed that a large proportion of the country's wealth was held by a small proportion of the population, hence the generalized term or expression, the 80/20 rule. Lorenz, early in the twentieth century and based on these observations, produced a cumulative graph for demonstrating the dominance of the '20 per cent'. Juran, in the 1950s, using a similar analogy, observed that a large proportion of quality problems were attributable to a small number of causes (i.e. 80 per cent of the rejections are caused by 20 per cent of the defect types).

The technique involves ranking the collected data, usually via a check sheet, with the most commonly occurring problem at the top and the least at the bottom. The contribution of each problem

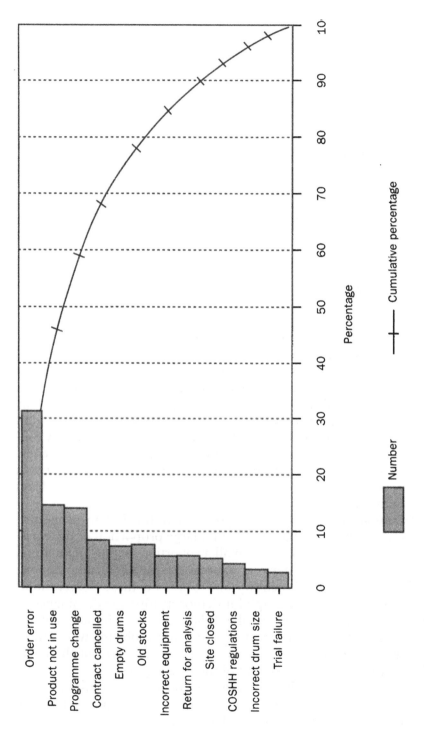

Figure 6.10 Pareto analysis: reasons for returned goods. *Source:* Betz Dearborn

to the grand total is expressed as a percentage, and cumulative percentages are used in compounding the effect of these problems. The ranking of the problems is usually in terms of occurrence and/or cost – just because one defect type happens more frequently than another it does not necessarily mean that it is the costliest or the one that should be tackled first. The results are often presented in two ways: (1) ranked data as a bar chart and (2) cumulative percentages as a graph. Figure 6.10 is an example from Betz Dearborn with respect to the reasons for returned goods.

Pareto analysis, while simple in terms of its construction, is extremely powerful in presenting data by focusing attention on the major contributor(s) to a quality problem in order to generate attention, efforts, ideas and suggestions and – it is hoped – gain a significant overall reduction in these problems. It is not a 'once and for all' analysis. If used regularly and consistently, the presentational part of the technique is extremely useful in demonstrating continuous improvement made over a period of time.

The following are the basic steps in constructing a Pareto diagram:

● Agree the problem that is to be analysed.
● Decide the time period over which data is to be collected.
● Identify the main causes or categories of the problem.
● Collect the data using, for example, a check sheet.
● Tabulate the frequency of each category and list in descending order of frequency (if there are too many categories it is permissible to group some into a miscellaneous category, for the purpose of analysis and presentation).
● Arrange the data in a bar graph format.
● Construct the Pareto diagram with the columns arranged in order of descending frequency.
● Determine cumulative totals and percentages and construct the cumulative percentage curve.

Difficulties associated with Pareto analysis are:

● Misrepresentation of the data.
● Inappropriate measurements depicted.
● Knowing when and how to use Pareto analysis.
● Lack of understanding of how it should be applied to particular problems.
● Inaccurate plotting of cumulative percentage data.

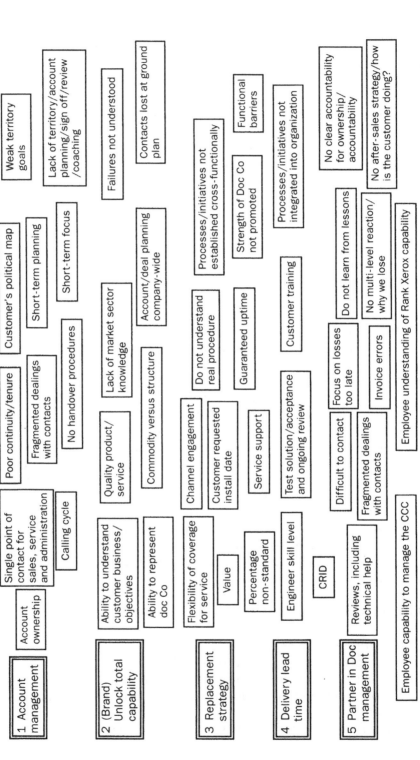

Figure 6.11 Relations diagram: linking issues and ideas from the affinity diagram relating to managing the customer contact cycle.
Source: Rank Xerox

Overcome the difficulties by:

- Defining clearly the purpose of the use of Pareto analysis for the problem to hand.
- Identifying the most appropriate measurement parameters.
- Using a check sheet or sheets to collect data for the likely major causes of the problem/project being investigated.
- Including details of the data sources with the completed analysis.
- Carefully scrutinizing the results.
- Asking whether the exercise has clarified the situation.

Relations Diagram

Relations diagrams are used to identify, understand and clarify complex cause and effect relationships to find the causes and solutions to a problem and to determine the key factors in the situation under study. They are also employed to identify the key issues to some desired result. Relations diagrams are used when the causes are non-hierarchical and when there are multiple interrelated problems. They allow the problem to be analysed from a wide perspective, because a specific framework is not employed. Relations diagrams can be considered to be a freer and broader version of a cause and effect diagram. Figure 6.11 is an example from Rank Xerox, which links the issues and ideas from the affinity diagram in figure 6.1 in relation to managing the CCC.

The major steps in constructing a relations diagram are:

- The central problem or issue to be discussed is described clearly and accepted by those concerned.
- Issues, causes and related problems that are believed to be affecting the central problem(s) are identified. These are written, in summary form, on cards, one issue, cause or problem per card.
- The cards are then placed around the central problem/issue in a cause and effect relationship. This is done by placing the card believed to have the strongest relationship closest to the central problem/issue; other cards are ranked accordingly.
- The cause and effect cards are enclosed within rectangles or ovals, and arrows are used to highlight which causes and effects are related. The relationship is indicated by arrows pointing

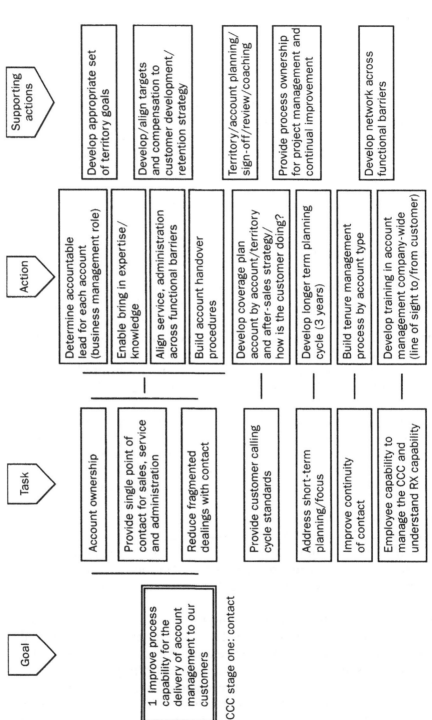

Figure 6.12 Systematic diagram: range of paths and tasks to be accomplished to manage customer retention. *Source:* Rank Xerox

from cause to effect. The key cause and effects are emphasized by double lines, shading etc.

- Appropriate revisions are made to the diagram.
- The resulting diagram is analysed for principle causes.

Difficulties associated with relationship diagrams are:

- Confusion with a cause and effect diagram in terms of to which type of problem it should be applied.
- Stifling logical patterns of thought.
- Questioning the credibility of the data that has been collected.
- The volume of data being handled and portrayed on the diagram, which may prevent focus on key items.

Overcome the difficulties by:

- Determining the key relationships by summing the number of incoming and outgoing arrows.
- Clearly indicating the major cause and effect relationships.
- Seeking the views of people from outside the team to assess the accuracy of the diagram.

Systematic Diagram

Systematic or tree diagrams are used to examine, in a systematic manner, the most appropriate and effective means of planning to accomplish a task ('how to') or solve a problem ('why'); events are represented in the form of a root and branch relationship. Such diagrams display in increasing detail the means necessary to achieve a specific goal or clarify the component parts that lead to the root cause of a problem. They are used when the causes that influence the problem are known, but a plan and method for resolving the problem have not been developed. Systematic diagrams are usually used to evaluate several different methods and plans for solving a problem and thereby assisting with complex implementations. They are also useful to identify dependencies in a given situation and to search for the most suitable improvement methods. Figure 6.12 is an example from Rank Xerox, which maps out the full range of paths and tasks to be accomplished to manage customer retention.

The major steps in constructing a systematic diagram are:

- The problem to be solved or task to be accomplished is written on a card. The card is placed on the left-hand side of the board, table, wall or other means being used to display the data.
- The primary methods and tasks to accomplish the objective or primary causes of the problem are identified. A typical question used in this identification is 'To achieve the objective, what are the key means?'. Each of these methods, tasks etc. is written on a card and placed directly to the right of the problem statement. In this way the first level of a root and branch relationship is created.
- Each primary method, task, idea, cause etc. is treated as the objective and the previous step repeated with these secondary methods etc. placed to the right of the ones to which they relate, in this way forming the tertiary level. This process is then repeated until all ideas are exhausted. It is unusual to go beyond four levels in development of the means.
- Working back from the right-hand side of the completed diagram through the levels, the relationship between objectives and means, or problem and causes, is checked to ensure that the means and causes are each related to the objectives and problem, respectively: 'Will such and such an objective be accomplished if a particular method or task is implemented?'

Difficulties associated with systematic diagrams are:

- A poorly defined primary goal or issue.
- Failure to identify all of the means to achieve the goals.
- Leaving gaps in the diagram as a result of inadequately answered questions.
- Allowing the diagram to become inflexible.

Overcome the difficulties by:

- Having clear, simple objectives or issues.
- Applying logical thinking.
- Using the combined experience of the team.
- Working to the level of detail decided by the team at the outset.
- Using the output for action planning (how to?) or root cause elimination; action planning (why?).

Summary

This chapter has demonstrated that a wide range of difficulties are likely to be encountered with even the simplest of tools. A number of common threads run through these difficulties, including a lack of knowledge and understanding of the fundamentals of a particular tool, incorrect application, failure to use the results and lack of teamwork.

The means of overcoming the typical difficulties encountered with each tool have been defined, and these can be classified into a number of broad headings, including: ensuring that those likely to be affected by the use of a tool are briefed on the purpose of the project being tackled and are included in the construction and use of the tool; checking at regular intervals that the tool is being used correctly; modifying, as appropriate, the basic construction of the tool; using the results and communicating the findings; ensuring that adequate training and education are undertaken and being clear on the purpose of using a particular tool. These means of counteracting the problems, although relatively simplistic in nature, are often not easy to put into practice.

7 An Overview of Common Techniques

Introduction

This chapter follows the same format as chapter 6, but concentrates on some of the more popular quality management techniques used in continuous improvement. Techniques are by their very nature more complex than tools in structure and application; for this reason, more discussion is devoted to each technique than was the case with tools in chapter 6.

Benchmarking

Benchmarking as it is known today originated in Rank Xerox. It is now well documented (e.g. Camp 1989) that when Rank Xerox started to evaluate its copying machines against the Japanese competition it found that the Japanese companies were selling their machines for what it cost Rank Xerox to make them. It was also assumed that the Japanese-produced machines were of poor quality; this was proved not to be the case. This exposure of the Corporation's vulnerability highlighted the need for change, which was led by David Kearns, who had then just been promoted to the position of CEO.

Benchmarking is defined by Rank Xerox as 'the continuous process of measuring products, services and processes against the strongest competitors or those renowned as world leaders in their field'. It was adopted by them in 1981 as a company-wide effort. Put simply, benchmarking is an opportunity to learn from the experience of others. Benchmarking helps to develop an improvement mindset among staff, it facilitates an understanding of best practices and processes, helps people to understand processes, challenges existing practices within the business and assists in setting goals. It is used whenever it is necessary to share an approach to change or improve business processes. Benchmarking is a key action evaluating many of the activities associated with self-assessment against a model of business excellence.

Most organizations carry out what can be termed informal benchmarking. This takes two main forms: (1) visits to other businesses to obtain ideas to facilitate improvements in one's own organization and (2) the collection, in a variety of ways, of data about competitors. This is often not done in any planned way; it is interesting but limited in its value.

To make the most effective use of benchmarking and use it as a learning experience as part of a continual process rather than a one-shot exercise, a more formal approach is required. However, before an organization embarks on formal benchmarking it is important that its staff are prepared to spend time understanding how their own processes work. This will often be the key criterion of the benchmarking activity.

There are three main types of formal benchmarking:

1 Internal benchmarking. This is the easiest form of benchmarking to conduct and involves benchmarking between businesses within the same group of companies. In this way, best practice and initiatives are shared across businesses.
2 Competitive benchmarking. This is a comparison against the direct competition. It is often difficult, if not impossible in some industries, to obtain the data for this form of benchmarking.
3 Functional/generic benchmarking. This is a comparison of specific processes with the 'best in class' in different industries. It is usually not difficult to obtain access to other organizations to perform this type of benchmarking. Organizations are often keen to swop and share information in a network or partnership arrangement.

There are a number of steps in a formal benchmarking process. They are now described briefly; more detail can be found in Camp (1989), McNair and Leibfreid (1993) and Watson (1992).

• Identify what is the subject to be benchmarked (e.g. the invoicing process) and reach agreement on the measures to be used (e.g. number of invoices per day, per person).

- Identify which companies will be benchmarked.
- Agree the most appropriate means of collecting the data, the type of data to be collected, who will be involved and a plan of action.
- Determine the reasons for the current gap (positive or negative) in performance between the company and the best among the companies involved in the benchmarking exercise.
- Estimate, over an agreed time frame, the change in performance of the company and the benchmark company in order to assess whether the gap is going to grow or decrease.
- Define and establish the goals to close or increase the gap in performance. This step requires effective communication of the benchmarking exercise findings.
- Develop action plans to achieve the goals. This step involves gaining acceptance of the plans by all employees likely to be affected by the changes.
- Implement the actions, plans and strategies. This involves effective project planning and management.
- Assess and report the results of the action plans.
- Reassessment or recalibration of the benchmark. This should be conducted on a regular and systematic basis and involves maintaining good links with the benchmark partners.

Difficulties associated with benchmarking are:

- Lack of planning, strategy and preparation in terms of setting up the benchmarking study, commissioning the team and agreeing the purpose of the study.
- Treating it in a superficial manner.
- Considering it as a way of reducing the number of people employed in a particular function.
- Failure to understand one's own processes prior to embarking on benchmarking.
- The subject of the benchmarking is not appropriate.
- Underestimation of the work involved.
- Incorrect identification of benchmarks.
- Lack of integration of benchmarking results into the business improvement process.
- Failure to follow all the stages of benchmarking in a structured manner.

- Inappropriate project sponsor and manager.
- Lack of commitment from team members.
- Inappropriate choice of benchmark partners.
- Lack of trust between benchmark partners.
- Data paralysis.
- The attitude that 'industrial tourism' is the same as formal benchmarking.
- An unwillingness to learn from others, in particular from those outside the 'industry' sector.
- Failure to address all of the issues arising from a benchmarking exercise.
- Failure to communicate the findings to operational personnel.
- Lack of review/sign off.
- Failing to abide by the benchmarking code of conduct.

Overcome the difficulties by:

- Clear project definition.
- Sticking to the objectives and treating benchmarking as a long-term project.
- Being realistic about the time required to complete the individual steps of the benchmarking project.
- Treating it as a continuous process and not as a one-off exercise, campaign or programme.
- Ensuring that benchmarking is linked to the objectives of the business.
- Management involvement and ongoing commitment and support.
- Understanding your own processes before seeking benchmarking data.
- Encouraging creativity and innovation.
- Ensuring that any comparisons made are valid.
- Ensuring that the members of the team undertaking the benchmarking project do not become insular and try to do everything themselves.
- Sharing information.
- Commitment to research and the implementation of new ideas.
- Assessing the effectiveness of the actions taken in response to benchmarking.
- Communicating the findings, outcomes and results.

Departmental Purpose Analysis

The main value of departmental purpose analysis (DPA) is facilitating the internal customer–supplier relationship, determining the effectiveness of departments, and extending the quality improvement initiatives to non-manufacturing areas. The concept of DPA originated at IBM (see Lewis (1984) for details). The key features of DPA are:

- A departmental task analysis is carried out to determine what needs to be achieved by a department in order to meet the company objectives. In this way, a department's objectives are aligned to company objectives. It helps to ensure uniformity of opinion on both departmental and company objectives.
- Determining, in a clear manner, the purpose, roles, responsibilities and total contribution of a department to adding value to an organization's activities; non-value-adding work is highlighted.
- Determining the workload of departmental staff and the current utilization of skills.
- Describing the relationship between a department and its internal customers/suppliers.
- Providing the basis for applying and establishing performance measures by which a department can ensure that it is focusing on satisfying the needs and expectations of its internal customers. From the measurements, improvement objectives and targets can be agreed with all those concerned.
- Identifying interdepartmental problems which can be the subject of a cross-functional improvement team.

An example of a DPA is given in figure 7.1 from the sales department of Betz Dearborn.

The following are the key steps in undertaking DPA:

- Define the purpose and aims of the department, and check that these are consistent with the Company's mission and vision.
- Draw up a list of the main tasks carried out within the department. Prioritize the tasks, agree this with departmental staff and confirm with line management.
- List the key skills and activities for each of the key tasks; a flow chart is a useful tool to assist with this. For each of these tasks, identify and list the customers and the suppliers.

- For each supplier identify what input they provide and who this originates from. For each customer determine what output they receive and who receives it.
- Discuss the inputs and outputs received from each supplier and customer, identify any irregularities and abnormalities, and agree specifications for needs.
- Identify any non-value-added time. This is defined as the time spent on tasks and activities that are carried out but that do not meet customer requirements first time and on tasks that are not required.
- Draw up an action plan to achieve agreed specifications and to reduce the non-value-added time.
- Review the skill requirements to identify any training needs.

Difficulties associated with DPA are:

- The purpose and aims of a department are not sufficiently defined.
- It is treated as a paperwork analysis and as a report to be filed away.
- Not all of the customers of a department are involved in its preparation.
- Inputs and outputs to a department are not clearly identified.
- The non-value-added activity identified from the analysis is not addressed.
- Functional and departmental barriers.

Overcome the difficulties by:

- Ensuring that the objectives of DPA are clear and well communicated.
- Involving all members of the department in developing a DPA.
- Ensuring that the department is clearly committed to assessing its own performance.
- Integrating with business process reengineering.
- Developing a package of performance measures to reflect the analysis and an appropriate monitoring mechanism.
- Developing a project-based improvement plan. This should be targeted at eliminating the non-value-added activity.
- Holding joint improvement team meetings with customers and suppliers.

(a) Main tasks – suppliers

Task	What is the input?	Who provides it?	Is it right?	How can it be modified?
Taking of orders	Phone calls, telexes, fax messages, ansafone, postal orders	Clients, salespersons, unit offices	In the main yes, but some aspects such as packaging sizes, address detail, order numbers, are sometimes given with the assumption we know what is missing.	Personnel placing orders could be more explicit with details. Some detail could be checked at unit offices prior to passing to sales office. Ansafone could be replaced by the Wang electronic mail system
Processing orders	Computer via visual display units and internal sales office order input form	Sales office	Yes, within our abilities and constant interruptions by phone calls and visitors, which by causing distractions can lead to errors.	A CSP is in the system to assist with efficiency. Sales department could specify if the checking of product programme is required as some require it and others do not
Answering enquiries and liaison with shipping and transport, warehousing and customer stores	Phone calls to Engineering Technical, Purchasing, Production, Credit Control, Customer Stores, Shipping and Transport, Warehousing	Clients, unit offices, Salespersons	Generally yes, but clients sometimes require miracles, and are annoyed and sometimes abusive if they do not get them.	Sales office is manned 9 a.m.–5 p.m. Technical back-up and stores are often not available during working day. Warehouse is unmanned after 4 p.m., which makes transport ineffective as they can only answer in the main based on information from the warehouse
Daily booked order figures	Edit list	Computer department	Yes	Computer could produce the same data but would have to run in parallel for one year while it built up a year's records.
Outstanding order list – chemicals	Computer listing 106	Computer department	No	Glassware and reagents should be on engineering list. Due date is required
Outstanding order list – engineering	Computer listing 109	Computer department	No	Glassware and reagents should be on this list, not on chemical list
New account raising	Orders	Clients, salespersons, unit offices	No	Sales office often get passed around in obtaining territory numbers; responsible sales units/offices should know their own prospects
Process confirmatory orders	Postal orders	Clients, unit offices, salespersons	No	These are confirmatory to verbal instructions. They are not required from unit offices and sales persons

(b) Main tasks–customers

Task	What is the output?	Who receives it?
Processing orders	A works order set	Warehouse stores, production control, purchasing and manufacturing plants
Answering enquiries and liaison with shipping and transport, warehousing and customer stores	Fast, accurate response	Clients, unit offices, salespersons, credit control, transport and stores
Daily booked order figures	Accurate booked sales figures	Sales management and operations management
Outstanding order list – chemicals	That all booked orders are progressed to invoices	Sales office
Outstanding order list – engineering	That all booked orders are progressed to invoices	Sales office
New account raising	The facility to process client orders	Sales office
Process confirmatory orders	Processed client orders	Sales office
Ordering and progress of engineering bought out items	Purchase requisitions and progress sheet	Engineering and purchasing departments
Price list maintenance	Special price lists	Sales office and sales management
Forward order diary	Orders raised to client's requirements	Sales office
Water treatment service and supervisory contracts	Memos annotated with account numbers and account special instruction facility displaying contract	Sales office and accounts department

Figure 7.1 Department purpose analysis: sales office. *Source:* Betz Dearborn

Design of Experiments

Design of experiments is a series of techniques that involve the identification and control of parameters or variables (termed factors) that have a potential impact on the performance and reliability of a product design and/or the output of a process, with the objective of optimizing product design, process design and process operation, and limiting the influence of noise factors. These techniques involve the identification and control of those parameters or variables (termed factors) that have a potential impact on the output of a process, the selection of two or more values (termed levels) of these variables and then running the process at these levels. Each combination or experimental run is known as a trial. The basic idea is to conduct a small number of experiments with different parameter values and analyse their effect on a defined output such as plating thickness. Based on the analysis, a prediction of system performance can be made. There are a number of methods of experimentation – trial and error (the one-at-a-time method), full factorial and fractional factorial.

The trial and error (or classical) method involves changing one factor at a time, keeping all other factors constant. The experiments are run until some optimum level is found for the single factor, then, keeping this factor at that level, variations are made to another factor to find its optimum with the other factors being kept constant and so on. Assumptions are then made about the preference for the lower or higher levels for each of the factors. This approach is familiar and easy to use and understand. However, it is widely criticized, not least for the fact that no information is provided about any interactions that may occur between the factors being tested leading to poor reproducibility. It is also inefficient, resource intensive and costly. In addition, it is not easy to hold, from experiment to experiment, the factors constant, and this in itself creates variation.

The full factorial approach is to consider all combinations of the factors that are being tested. In this way all possible interactions between the factors are investigated and the best combination identified. This may be feasible for a small number of factors but even with, say, seven factors at two levels, the minimum number of trials would be 2^7, i.e. 128. Despite the fact that both the main effects and interactions can be measured in a thorough and purely scientific manner, the time and costs associated with running such a large number of experiments are usually consider to be prohibitive and it is simply unrealistic in industrial situations. Also, much of the information obtained from the trials would be from combinations of factors that are of little practical use. This problem may be overcome by the use of fractional factorial designs.

Fractional factorial designs assume that higher order interactions are negligible and consequently the number of trials is a fraction of the full factorial (e.g. half or quarter). However, they still have the disadvantage of requiring a relatively large number of trials. Design of experiments dates back to the work for agricultural research of Sir R. A. Fisher in the 1920s and historically required a great deal of statistical knowledge and understanding, which most users found somewhat intimidating. Much effort has been devoted to simplifying the task. In the late 1970s, the work of Genichi Taguchi on experimental design made what is regarded by many as a major breakthrough in its application (see Taguchi (1986) for details of his method). Taguchi (1986), along with others (e.g. Plackett and Burman 1946), developed a series of orthogonal arrays to address the size of the experiment and thus aid the efficiency of conducting fractional factorial experiments. For example, the number of trials for seven factors at two levels would be reduced from 2^7 to (2^3). However, while economies in the design of experiment are achieved, there is an inevitable loss of information, usually about some possible interactions between factors. Despite this drawback most practitioners appear to favour the Taguchi approach. Not only are his methods cost effective and time efficient but they also work.

Taguchi is a statistician and electrical engineer, who was involved in rebuilding the Japanese telephone system, and who has been involved in applying design of experiments in the Japanese electronics industry for over 25 years. He promotes three distinct stages of designing-in quality:

- System design: the basic configuration of the system is developed. This involves the selection of parts and materials and the use of feasibility studies and prototyping.
- Parameter design: the numerical values for the system variables (product and process parameters – factors) are chosen so that the system performs well, no matter what disturbances or noises (i.e. uncontrollable variables) are encountered by

the system (i.e. robustness). The experimentation pinpoints this combination of product/process parameter levels. The emphasis in parameter design is on using low-cost materials and processes in the production of the system. Parameter design is the key stage of designing-in quality. The objective is to identify optimum levels for these control factors so that the product and/or process is least sensitive to changes in the noise factors.

- Tolerance design: if the system is not satisfactory, then tolerance design is then used to improve performance (i.e. reduce variation) by tightening the tolerances on those factors that have the largest impact on variation.

Taguchi's 'off-line' approach to quality control is well accepted in the West, in particular, with the engineering fraternity, but inevitably there are many criticisms of some of his statistical methods and, rather surprisingly, of the advocated philosophy. What the critics seem to forget is that Taguchi's methods have proven successful, both in Japan and the West, and those organizations that have adopted his methods have succeeded in making continuous improvement. It is this which is important and not the methods used. There is little doubt that his work has led to increased interest in a variety of approaches and methodologies relating to design of experiments.

An example of a design of experiments on liner bond strength carried out at Rexam Corrugated South West Ltd is given in figure 7.2.

The key steps in designing and running a fractional factorial experiment are:

- Step 1: decide and define the project objective. This should include, the provision of a statement of interest, objectives to be achieved and performance to be addressed.
- Step 2: select critical characteristics. The critical factors that affect performance (e.g. temperature, pressure, speed and the percentage of constituents making up a product or mix of material) and can improve performance (e.g. plating thickness) need to be identified, along with the interactions that can affect performance. The preparation of a cause and effect diagram and/or affinity diagram may aid this identification. This step should be undertaken by people who are knowledgeable about the process under investigation; this would be done using engineering

	Gap	Straw unwind	Gaylord heater	Fluting shower	Liner wrap	Small P/heat	Roll pressure	Strength	Variation
Set 1	6	Off	On	Off	Off	Off	40	58.73	6.93
Set 2	6	Off	On	On	On	On	60	76.27	7.18
Set 3	6	On	Off	Off	Off	On	60	63.26	6.29
Set 4	6	On	Off	On	On	Off	40	67.07	7.53
Set 5	9	Off	Off	Off	On	Off	60	61.65	4.51
Set 6	9	Off	Off	On	Off	On	40	61.19	4.90
Set 7	9	On	On	Off	On	On	40	65.56	4.57
Set 8	9	On	On	On	Off	Off	60	62.73	5.41

(Grade: 17FKB4, Speed: 140 M/min)

Figure 7.2 Design of experiments: Liner bond strength. *Source*: Rexam Corrugated South West Ltd

'know-how', with some form of instinctive 'gut feeling'. From this, those factors that appear to be sensible for experimentation are selected.

- Step 3: determine the issues that affect the critical characteristics.
- Step 4: identify and list the control and noise factors. Control factors are those factors that may be controlled during production (e.g. temperature, speed, tension, pressure and material type). Noise factors are those factors that are difficult or impossible to control in production. They include atmospheric conditions, ageing of equipment, machine maintenance, operator skills and shift differences. A fundamental part of parameter design is to experiment with the control factors that are to be tested against the noise conditions likely to be experienced in practice. The control factors that are to be optimized during the experiment need to be selected as part of this step.
- Step 5: select the control factors to be optimised during the experiment.
- Step 6: choose the orthogonal array and assign factors to columns. Establish the levels at which each factor is to be tested. From the number of factors, possible interactions and number of levels, identify the orthogonal array to be used in the experiment. There are a number of popular arrays, with perhaps seven covering most applications. Decide which factors are to be placed in each column of the orthogonal array. It is

usual to place control factors that are more difficult to change in the first and second columns on the left hand side of the array. Sometimes deciding what to allocate to columns is not straightforward, especially when interactions are to be studied. The rows and columns of the orthogonal array form the experimental plan.

- Step 7: choice of sample size. The sample size for the experiment should be sufficient to ensure that the noises have an opportunity to have an influence on the various control factor combinations governed by the orthogonal array.
- Step 8: organize the experiment and carry it out. This often involves considerable organization and logistics in tracking the products involved in the experiment.
- Step 9: analyse and interpret the results, looking for relevant interactions.
- Step 10: carry out a confirmation run at the optimum settings to validate the conclusions.

Some suggested reading, in addition to Taguchi (1986): Barker (1990), Bendell et al. (1989) and Lochnar and Matar (1990).

Difficulties associated with design of experiments are:

- Uncertainty about how to set about conducting an experiment.
- Poor understanding of the concept and its underlying methods, and the associated lack of confidence.
- Underestimating the time allowed for the experiment.
- Deciding which are the key factors and main interactions to be investigated, along with setting appropriate levels for the factors.
- Poor understanding of the operating characteristics inherent in the production equipment, in particular those controlling devices that are easy or difficult to increase and decrease.
- Separating control and noise factors.
- Deciding on the sample size to ensure that the noise in the system will have the opportunity to act upon the control factors.
- Determining whether or not factors are independent and deciding the key interactions to be tested.
- Availability of products and materials used in the experiment.
- Inaccuracies arising from the measurement equipment.
- Interpreting the results and assessing their significance.

Overcome the difficulties by:

- Involving people who are knowledgeable about the process in the experimental design.
- In the beginning do not be ambitious; use the less complex arrays.
- Attempting to keep jargon to a minimum.
- Undertaking a number of small experiments in a step-by-step manner.
- Maintaining throughout the experiment an alert investigative manner, both to the nature of the problem being investigated and the resulting data.
- Carrying out the experiment in a controlled manner without disrupting production.
- Using software to undertake the necessary calculations.
- Acting on the results of the experiment and putting in place a system for monitoring the reproducibility of experimental results.

Failure Mode and Effects Analysis

The technique of failure mode and effects analysis (FMEA) was developed in the aerospace and defence industries. It is a systematic and analytical quality planning tool for identifying, at the product, service and process design stages, what potentially could go wrong either with a product during its manufacture or end use by the customer or with the provision of a service. FMEA is a powerful aid to undertaking advanced quality planning of new products and services, since it assists in the development of robust and reliable production and delivery methods. Its effective use should lead to reductions in:

- defects during the production of initial samples and in volume production
- customer complaints
- failures in the field
- performance-related deficiencies
- warranty claims

There are two categories of FMEA: design and process. Design FMEA assesses what could, if not corrected, go wrong with the product in service and during manufacture as a consequence of a weakness in the design. When used in this way it assists in the identification or confirmation of critical characteristics. Process FMEA is mainly concerned with the reasons for potential failure during manufacture and in service as a result of non-compliance with the original design intent, or failure to achieve the design specification.

From the design FMEA, the potential causes of failure should be studied and actions taken before designs and drawings are finalized. Likewise, with the process FMEA, actions must be put into place before the process is set up. Used properly, FMEA prevents potential failures occurring in the manufacturing, producing and/or delivery processes or in the end-product during use, and will ensure that processes, products and services are more robust and reliable. There is little doubt that a number of the well-publicized product-recall campaigns that occur every year could conceivably be avoided by the effective use of FMEA. However, it is important that FMEA is seen not just as a catalogue of potential failures, but as a technique for pursuing quality improvement. It should not be viewed as a paperwork exercise carried out to retain business, because this will limit its perceived usefulness.

The concept, procedures and logic involved with FMEA are not new; every forward-thinking design, planning and production engineer and technical specialist carries out, in an informal manner, various aspects of FMEA. In fact, most people in their daily routines will subconsciously use a simple, informal FMEA. However, this mental analysis is rarely committed to paper in a format that can be evaluated by others and discussed as the basis for a corrective action plan. What FMEA does is to provide a planned, systematic method of capturing and documenting this knowledge; it also forces people to use a disciplined approach and is a vehicle for obtaining collective knowledge and experience through team activity.

Details of FMEA are provided in Dale (1994) and Ford Motor Company (1988).

The procedure involved in the development of FMEA is progressive iteration. In brief, it involves the following steps:

- Form a team.
- Flow chart the details of the relevant part, product, service or process that is under study.

- Identify the function of the part, product, service and/or process and enter onto the FMEA form suitable details of the part, product, assembly, service etc. which is under analysis.
- Identify potential failure modes in the part, product, service etc. Each potential failure mode for the part and part function should be listed. Data on previous parts is a useful starting point.
- The effects of each potential failure on the customer (internal and external) should be described and assessed.
- The causes of potential failure should be examined, with each failure cause assigned to a failure mode.
- The likelihood that a specific cause will result in the failure mode is estimated.
- The current controls are reviewed and the ability to detect a potential failure mode in relation to potential design, service or process weakness is assessed.
- Determine a risk priority number (RPN). This comprises an assessment of (1) occurrence, (2) detection and (3) severity of ranking and is the sum of the three rankings:
  - The occurrence is the likelihood of a specific cause that will result in the identified failure mode, based on perceived or estimated probability ranked on a scale of 1–10.
  - The detection criterion relates, in the case of a design FMEA, to the likelihood of the design verification programme pinpointing a potential failure mode before it reaches the customer. A ranking of 1–10 is used. In the process FMEA, this relates to the existing control plan.
  - The severity of effect on a scale of 1–10 indicates the likelihood of the customer noticing any difference to the functionality of the product or service.

  The resulting RPN should always be checked against past experience of similar products, services and situations. After it has been determined, the potential failure modes in descending order of RPN should be the focus for improvement action to reduce/eliminate the risk of failure occurring.
- Corrective action to be taken to help eliminate potential concerns is recommended. This, along with the countermeasures that have been put in place, is monitored.

The requisite information and actions are recorded on a standard FMEA form. See figure 7.3 for a process FMEA from Allied Signal TurboChargers.

Process _____ Turbo A ssr 452038/9 – 1
Product name/part no _____ Turbo TB2544
MD/process responsibility _____ Manuf Dept GAL
Other MD(s)/involved _____ Garrett SA
Outside suppliers affected? Yes_____

Part name(s) Part no. vendor(s)	Process operation reference function	Potential failure mode	Potential effect(s) of failure	Potential cause(s) of failure
Turbine housing arm and valve assembly bushing	Fit bush and arm valve assembly to turbine housing	Bush out of position	Low boost	Assay variation
		Arm jams in bush	Valve sticks, high, low boost	Mis-alignment of arm and bush
Valve assembly, crank assembly	Weld crank assembly	Weld fails	Low boost	Eccentric weld, incorrect weld parameters
Crank assembly	Weld crank assembly	Low end float	Valve sticks, high, low boost, arm seizure	Worn feeler strip, feeler strip not used
		Incorrect crank angle	Difficult calibration, poor performance	Incorrect weld set up, setting variation
		Incorrect orientation	Induced stress on centre housing oil connections	Assembly variation
THWA, CHRA, clamp, bolt, seal ring	Assemble THWA to CHRA and compressor seal ring	Loose bolts	Audible gas leak, oil pull over, rub induced noise	Low torque, assembly tool incorrectly set
Compressor housing elbow fitting	Compressor housing sub assembly	Fitting comes loose	High boost	Low torque, assembly tool incorrectly set

Figure 7.3 Failure mode and effects analysis for processes. *Source*: Allied Signal TurboChargers

SQA or manuf eng _____S Hart/ J Aldridge_____ ext _____

Sign below

_____

Product engineer _____ ext _____

_____

Application engineer _____R Mover_____ ext _____

_____

Sched job no _____WI 711_____

FMEA data orig _____17 Apr 90_____ rev _13 Jun 90_ Page _1_ of _3_

Existing conditions				Recommended action(s) and status	Responsible fort action and date	Resulting			
Current or foreseen controls	Occurrence	Severity	Detection	RRN risk priority no.			Action(s) taken and date	Occurrence	Severity	Detection
Bush position gauge, operator gauge check 1 in 10	7	7	9	441	Carry out capability study on first assembly build – Report no. 90/22 indicated process improvement still required by Manufacturing	Manufacturing and quality assurance	Report no. 90/022 (452039−1) Cpk=−0.46 Cp=0.11 100% gauging to be used until process capable	7	7	9
Operator check for free movement	2	7	3	42						
Initial set up, met lab sectional test, operator visual, weld control settings	7	7	9	441	Reassess RPN following ISIR and capability study	Manufacturing and quality assurance				
Operator vigilance, physical check for end float and valve function by operator	2	7	9	126	Carry out capability study on ISIR batch Report no. 90/022 Cpk=0 12 Cp=0.3 further study required. Carry out capability study on cmm	Manufacturing and quality assurance	Report no. 90/032 (452039−1) Cpk=−0.37 Cp=1.14 End float gauge introduced. GG2249 100% check required			
Operator checks initial parts on set up. QA audit check	3	7	8	168		Manufacturing and quality assurance		2	7	8
First off by QA. Initial set up. QA audit	6	6	3	108	Carry out capability study on cmm	Manufacturing and quality assurance	Report no. 90/032 (450239−1) Cpk=1.47 Cp=1.56			
100 per cent check. QA audit, torque tool calibration by quality assurance	2	7	7	98		Manufacturing and quality assurance				
Method of assembly, 100 per cent visual over check by quality assurance	2	7	2	28						

Difficulties associated with FMEA are:

- It can be viewed by engineers and technical staff as a catalogue of failures and as a paperwork exercise to satisfy the contractual demands of customers.
- Allocating sufficient time to prepare the necessary details.
- Availability of team members.
- Undertaken in isolation by key staff without seeking the views of others as part of a structured and disciplined team approach.
- Too large or too small a team used for the preparation of an FMEA and the wrong people being members of the team.
- FMEA meetings getting bogged down.
- Tiresome task of writing up the analysis.
- The project addressed is too large.
- The overlap between the design and process FMEA is not recognized.
- Applying FMEA with little emphasis placed on positive corrective actions to reduce potential failure modes. Similarly, problem areas may be identified or recommended actions developed but not addressed.
- Being prepared retrospectively or after the design or process has been finalized.

Overcome the difficulties by:

- Sanctioning FMEA by senior management to emphasize among engineering and technical staff that it should be used as part of their day-to-day job.
- Outlining its use to the team prior to commencing the preparation of an FMEA.
- Ensuring that team members are knowledgeable about the product, system or process under examination.
- To prevent inefficient use, the analysis should be carried out under the control of a knowledgeable team leader/facilitator.
- Transfer of experiences from previous FMEA.
- Having a mechanism or structure to eliminate, in turn, each potential failure mode.
- Regarding the FMEA as a 'live' document and updating it on a continuous basis.
- Management must respond positively to the suggested improvement actions arising from an FMEA exercise.

Mistake-Proofing

Mistake-proofing (poka yoke) is a technique that is used to prevent an error being converted into a defect. The concept was developed by Shingo (1986). The technique is based on the assumption that no matter how observant or skilled people are, mistakes will occur unless preventive measures are put in place. Shingo argues that using statistical methods is tantamount to accepting defects as inevitable, and that instead of looking for and correcting the causes of defective work, the source of the mistake should be inspected, analysed and rectified. He places great emphasis on what he calls source inspection, which checks for factors that cause mistakes, and then using mistake-proofing devices to prevent their recurrence.

Mistake-proofing has two main steps: preventing the occurrence of a defect and detecting the defect. Depending on the application, mistake-proofing devices can be applied at three points in the process:

1 in the event of an error, prevent the start of a process,
2 prevent a non-conforming product from leaving a process, and
3 prevent a non-conforming part being passed to the next process.

A typical example of a mistake-proofing device provided by Nissan Motor Manufacturing UK is given in figure 7.4.

The mistake-proofing technique employs the ingenuity and skills not only of the engineers and/or technical specialists, who may develop and fit the devices, but also of the operators who may have first identified the cause of the mistake and participated in the corrective action measures. In Japanese companies, Quality Control Circles are very active in developing and using mistake-proofing devices. The devices may be simple mechanical counters, which ensure that the correct number of parts is fed into a machine; they may be cut-off switches, limit switches or float switches, which provide some regulatory control of the process or operation, thereby stopping a machine or process automatically. They may be devices that prevent a part being incorrectly fed into the machine, assembled incorrectly, fabricated incorrectly, or placed incorrectly into fixturing. In other words, the assumption is made that, if the part can possibly be fed in wrongly, etc. it will be unless some preventive measure is taken. This is the essence of

Operation: Welding exhaust pipe to silencer
Requirements: The silencer must be fitted with the manufacturer's embossed
                name on the same side of every assembly

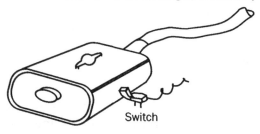

Concern: The silencer is elliptical in section and can be located on to the
                welding jig with the embossed name either way up
Poka yoke: A proximity switch is fitted in the circuit of the welder which must
                be activated by contacting the rolled seam (only on one side of
                the silencer) before the welding operation may commence

Figure 7.4 Mistake-proofing device. *Source*: Nissan Motor Manufacturing UK Ltd

mistake-proofing. It is usual to integrate the mistake-proofing device with some audible signal, visual display or warning light to indicate that something has gone wrong.

The following are the key steps in mistake-proofing:

- Study potential problems and the likely causes of mistakes. An FMEA is a useful starting point.
- Undertake basic training in the principles, tools and concepts of mistake-proofing.
- Decide whether a formal team approach is to be used for mistake-proofing and/or whether its use should be encouraged in a more informal manner.
- In preparing a mistake-proofing solution consult previously designed mechanisms and applications.
- Monitor the effectiveness of the mistake-proofing devices.

Difficulties associated with mistake proofing are:

- Engineers and technical staff are dismissive of the devices created by operators.
- Operating staff do not see it as their responsibility.
- Engineers claim that they do not have the time to design and produce the devices.
- The lack of on-site facilities to manufacture the devices.

Overcome the difficulties by:

- Getting engineers to develop devices for new products and encouraging operators and improvement teams to do the same with existing products.
- Making available some basic facility to allow people to construct and experiment with mistake-proofing devices.
- Recording details of successful applications in both the company and elsewhere and making them available at relevant parts of the plant.
- Mistake-proofing at the earliest opportunity, if possible at the development of a product and process.

Quality Costing

The investment required to introduce and sustain a process of continuous and company-wide improvement can be considerable. The majority of managements are not used to committing expenditure as a blind act of faith and usually wish to check that the investment is cost effective. Quality costing can be used to make this assessment. It also assists in monitoring the effectiveness of the improvement efforts and initiatives being undertaken. It is not easy to do, but those organizations that have persisted in defining quality costs and then monitoring and reducing them have gained benefits from the process.

Quality costing expresses an organization's quality performance in the language of senior management, shareholders and financial institutions – money. It is often found that senior management are unmoved by quality assurance data but are spurred into action when the same data are expressed and presented in monetary terms, in particular when the cost of quality as a percentage of annual sales turnover is of the same order as profit. Operators and first-line management are also found to react positively to quality initiatives when non-conformance data are presented in these terms.

The benefits of quality costs are related to their uses, and these are both numerous and diverse. They include:

- Promoting quality as a business parameter.
- Helping to keep quality aspects of the business under the spotlight.
- Enabling business decisions about quality to be made in an objective manner.
- Helping to identify and justify investment in prevention-based activities, equipment and tooling.
- Educating staff in the concept of TQM as a key business parameter and thereby gaining their commitment and reducing scepticism.
- Facilitating performance measurement.
- Identifying products, processes and departments for investigation.
- Focusing attention on the problems for which compensation has already been built into the system.
- Assisting in setting cost-reduction targets and measuring progress towards these targets.
- Providing a base for budgeting and eventual cost control.

The main approaches to quality cost collection are described by Dale and Plunkett (1995) and include:

- The list of cost elements typically described in BS.6143 (1990) and Campanella (1990).
- A list of elements developed from company-specific experience and the literature.
- The use of semi-structured methods, including the process cost model outlined in BS.6143 (1992).

The elements identified from any of these approaches can be based on people's activities and/or material waste.

The following are the first steps by which an organization can approach the collection, analysis and reporting of quality costs:

- It is unlikely that an organization's management accounts will contain the necessary information in the right form. Hence it is essential to involve accountants right from the outset.
- The purpose of quality costing should be clarified at the start because this may influence the strategy of the exercise. If, for

example, the main objective of the exercise is to identify high-cost problem areas, approximate costs will suffice. If, on the other hand, the purpose is to set a percentage cost-reduction target on the organization's total quality-related costs, it will be necessary to identify and measure all of the contributing cost elements in order to be sure that costs are reduced and not simply transferred elsewhere.

- It is necessary to decide how to deal with overheads, since many quality-related costs are normally included as part of the overhead, while others are treated as direct costs and attract a proportion of overheads. Failure to clarify this can lead to a gross distortion of the picture derived from the analysis. It is also easy to fall into the trap of double counting. For these and other reasons quality-related costs should be made the subject of a memorandum account. Another issue to be decided is how costs are to be allocated to components, material, etc. that are scrapped.

- Another area of difficulty is deciding whether some activities, usually of a setting-up, testing or running-in type, are quality activities or an integral and essential part of the production/operations activity. These costs often can be substantial and can alter the relative proportions of quality-related costs categories. There are also factors that help to ensure the basic utility of the product and/or service, guard against errors, and protect and preserve product and service quality. Examples are the use of design codes, preparation of engineering, technical and administrative systems and procedures, capital premiums on machinery and equipment, document and drawing controls, and handling and storage practices. Whether such factors give rise to costs that may be regarded as being quality-related is a matter for judgement in individual cases. These problems should be discussed with purchasing, engineering, production/operations and accountancy personnel, as appropriate, in order to resolve them.

- One of the maxims of quality cost collection seems to be that, in general, costs need to be large to hold the attention of people. Size is often regarded as being synonymous with importance, although it is size coupled with relevance and potential for reduction that determines the real importance of costs. Clearly, it may be much more advantageous to pursue a small percentage in a large cost than a large reduction in a small cost. This creates something of a dilemma for the cost collector because large costs are often insensitive to changes, but the collector canot omit large costs and concentrate only on smaller costs that may be readily seen to change. Hence cost groupings need to be chosen carefully so that the cost reductions achieved are displayed in such a way that both the relative achievement and absolute position are clearly shown. Another dilemma facing the cost collector arises from the fact that one-off estimates of quality costs tend not to change and some quality management specialists take the view that there is no point in collecting costs that do not change. The only way out of this dilemma is to measure directly, or through surrogates, those costs which it is thought worth collecting.

- A checklist of quality cost elements can provide a useful starting point for the cost collection exercise; however, there is no substitute for a thorough analysis of all of an organization's activities.
- In the absence of an established quality-related cost reporting system, start by looking into failure costs, specifically:
  - failure costs attributable to suppliers or subcontractors,
  - in-house mistakes, scrap, rework and remakes, and rectification costs,
  - downgraded products or 'seconds',
  - free repairs or replacements for products or services that are defective as delivered,
  - warranty and guarantee costs, and
  - litigation costs.
- Follow this by inquiring into the costs of inspection, checks, false starts, disruption to routine production and operations activities, and quality-related inefficiencies built into standard costs. Record how quality-related costs are computed so that the validity of comparisons made across departments, products, processes or time may be checked.
- When cost information is available, analyse it. Attribute costs to department, defect type, product, cause, supplier etc. Identify responsibility for costs with functions and people. Rank problems and cost reduction projects by size and importance. Integrate the collection, analysis and reporting of quality-related costs into the company accounting system – but aim to keep paperwork to a minimum.
- The reporting of quality costs should be such that the costs make an impact and the data is used to its full potential.

Difficulties associated with quality costing are:

- Many organizations have used quality costing to provide the launchpad for a process of improvement, but do not understand the potential barriers that enable accurate and consistent data to be collected, used and reported.
- Departmental managers giving a low priority to the identification and measurement of costs.
- Abandoning quality costing after the first few years. This means that there has been insufficient time to see significant reductions in the cost of quality, failure and wastage.
- The communication barrier which separates the professional accountant from the non-accountant.
- It is often discovered that the accounting system is unable to put a cost on the quality cost elements that have been decided upon, because of its structure or because of the lack of data, the so-called intangibles.
- The matter of definitions is crucial. Deciding what constitutes a quality cost and what cost is part of production/operating practice are the main issues.
- Determining which activities/costs are 'prevention, appraisal or failure'.
- Deciding on the level of accuracy of costs to be collected.
- Concerns about how to use the analysed cost data effectively.
- Large (or macro) costs are not sufficiently specific to allow ownership or give significant direction to the organization's improvement efforts.

Overcome the difficulties by:

- Establishing clear and concise objectives for quality cost collection.
- Concentrating on consistency rather than 100 per cent coverage and accuracy.
- Displaying the price of non-conformance, i.e. appraisal and failure, under the 'profit' figure on the regular monthly management information.
- Recognizing that quality costing is a management and not an accounting technique.
- Encouraging its use at department level as a means for facilitating improvement rather than something that is perceived to be administered by the financial department.
- Being clear on what constitutes a definition of a quality cost.
- Getting the purpose and strategy of the quality costing exercise clear at the outset.

- Not making comparisons unless comparability can be guaranteed.
- Getting data and costs from standard data wherever possible.
- Avoiding getting bogged down with trying to understand all of the underlying details.
- Ensuring that any first-off quality costing is soundly based.
- Indicating all existing cost sources in reports, including those that may not be currently quantifiable.
- Avoiding a multiplicity of quality costing reports.
- Exercising caution in the choice of ratios used to assess changes in quality costs.

Quality Function Deployment

The Quality Function Deployment (QFD) methodology was developed in Japan at Kobe Shipyard, Mitsubishi Heavy Industries. It arose out of a need to achieve simultaneously a competitive advantage in quality, cost and delivery (QCD). All of the leading companies in Japan use QFD. It is based on the philosophy that the 'voice of the customer' drives all company operations. The technique seeks to identify those features of a product or service that satisfy the real needs and requirements of customers (market or customer required quality). This analysis also takes into account discussions with the people who actually use the product, to obtain data on issues such as:

- How they feel about existing products,
- What bothers them,
- What features new products should have, and
- What is required to satisfy their needs, expectations, thinking and ideas.

It is usual to express the customer needs in the customers' original words and then translate these needs into the technical language of the organization. The superior performing companies use QFD to identify product and service features (including additional features) that customers will find attractive, and that will help to 'charm and delight them'. In this way differentiating quality characteristics, features and/or technical advantages can be established between the organization and its competition. These requirements, features and specifications are then translated into design requirements and subsequently deployed through each phase in the 'manufacturing' cycle to ensure that what is delivered to customers truly reflects their wants or needs. It provides the mechanism to target selected areas where improvement would enhance competitive advantage.

QFD is a systematic procedure to help build in quality in the upstream processes and in the early stage of new product development. In this way it helps to avoid problems in the downstream production and delivery processes and shortens the new product/service development time. It promotes proactive rather than reactive development.

Some of the major decisions that have to be made before QFD can be used include:

- Deciding which functions should be represented on the team and who is to be team leader, at the product planning stage.
- Overcoming the usual issues of team members saying they are too busy to attend team meetings, so that the team fails to meet on a regular basis. The need for good teamwork practices should also be recognized.
- Ensuring that the supporting tools and techniques are in place before QFD is used.

QFD employs a step-by-step approach from customer needs and expectations through the four planning phases of:

- product planning
- product development
- process planning
- production planning through to manufactured products and delivered services

In endeavouring to meet the objective of delighting the customer, conflicting issues often arise and some trade-offs are made in a logical manner.

An example of the 'house of quality' derived from the product planning phase of QFD, with respect to a turbocharger product from Allied Signal TurboChargers, is shown in figure 7.5. In simple terms, QFD comprises:

- The project to be studied should be identified and defined by management. The scope of the project should be clearly

1. Product planning

Product	Turbocharger
Model	T-X

Customer needs — Importance
- 1 – Minimal
- 2 – Minor
- 3 – Desirable
- 4 – Necessary
- 5 – Mandatory

Correlation
- ● Strong possibility
- ◆ Positive
- X Negative
- XX Strong negative

Product requirements — Relationships
- ● Strong – 6
- ○ Medium – 3
- ▲ Weak – 1

Customer satisfaction — Satisfaction
- 1 – Poor
- 2 – Fair
- 3 – Average
- 4 – Good
- 5 – Excellent

Relationship matrix

(● Strong, ○ Medium, ◆ Positive)

Customer need	Requirement	Importance rating	Turbine performance	Compressor performance	Product durability	Lube system integrity	Vibration resistance	Actuator durability	C.H.R.A. balance	Regulator calibration	Operating noise	Bearing system durability	No coking conditions	Mounting system integrity
Good power	Adequate amount	3	●	●	●			●		●		○		○
Good power	Fast response	5	○	○	●			●		○		○		◆
Good power	Smooth response	4	●	○	●							○		○
Good power	Low end response	4	●	●	●			●		●		○		◆
Good power	Low fuel usage	4	●	●				●		○				◆
No leaks	Air/exhaust	4				●	●							●
No leaks	Oil/water	4				○	○						○	
Reliable product	Safe product	5				●	●						●	○
Reliable product	No break down	5		○	●		●	●	○	●	○	●	●	●
Reliable product	No turbo noise	4	◆	○	●		○		●		●	●		●
Reliable product	No exhaust emissions	5	○				●	●		●				●

Customer satisfaction — Products compared

Requirement	T	A	B	C	Disadvantage
Adequate amount	3	3	4	4	
Fast response	4	4	3	3	
Smooth response	4	4	4	3	Y
Low end response	3	3	5	3	
Low fuel usage	3	3	3	3	
Air/exhaust	4	4	3	4	
Oil/water	2	1	2	4	Y
Safe product	3	3	3	3	
No break down	3	4	2	4	Y
No turbo noise	2	4	3	5	Y
No exhaust emissions	4	4	4	4	

Product requirement (Relationships x cust. need imp.)

	C1	C2	C3	C4	C5	C6	C7	C8	C9	C10	C11	C12	
Relationship totals	122	120	156	69	132	156	39	129	39	102	42	121	

Product requirement specifications — Proprietary

Rating scale:
1 – Poor
2 – Fair
3 – Average
4 – Good
5 – Excellent

Technical product evaluations — Performance ratings for product requirements

Products	C1	C2	C3	C4	C5	C6	C7	C8	C9	C10	C11	C12	Est. cost
A–2	3	3	3	4	3	5	1	5	5	3	3	4	360
B–4	5	3	4	4	3	3	2	3	2	5	4	3	285
C–6	3	4	3	5	5	4	4	4	4	4	3	4	345
T–7	3	4	3	4	2	3	5	3	1	4	3	4	330
T–X (Improved)	5	5	4	4	5	4	5	4	5	5	4	4	270

Quality history

	C1	C2	C3	C4	C5	C6	C7	C8	C9	C10	C11	C12
Field repairs – quantity / 1000	1.5	1.5	5.0	1.4	0.9	3.4			2.5	5.0	4.0	2.7
Warranty cost – cost / unit sold	.22	.17	.35	.24	.02	.60			.32	.45	.27	.18
Customer rejects – quantity / 1000									2.5			
Internal quality costs / unit sold							.10	.05	.50			

Evaluation summary

Relative rank:
1 – Low
2 – Medium
3 – High

	C1	C2	C3	C4	C5	C6	C7	C8	C9	C10	C11	C12	Weights
Product requirement importance (1,3,5)	5	5	5	3	5	5	1	5	1	3	1	5	60%
Competitive disadvantage – after improvement actions				Y		Y		Y					
Quality problems (1,3,5)	3	3	5	3	3	5	1	1	3	5	5	3	20%
Technical difficulty (1,3,5)	3	3	5	3	5	5	1	3	1	5	5	1	20%
Overall product requirement importance	4	4	5	3	5	4	1	4	3	4	3	4	

Figure 7.5 Quality function deployment. *Source: Allied Signal TurboChargers*

outlined, including targets and operating constraints. From this, a clearly-defined mission statement should be produced.

- Translate customer objectives and 'wants' (termed a 'what') into product or service design 'hows' (i.e. the product planning and design concept – phase 1). This 'voice of the customer' is the starting point for QFD and drives the process. Comparative analysis is performed between competitive products and/or services. This helps to rate the importance of each customer want (the outputs from this rating process are termed 'whys'). There may be conflicts between customer 'wants' and design requirement 'hows'. The centre relationship matrix of the chart represents the relationship strength of each customer need (whats) with each of the design requirement (hows). These conflicts are prioritized and a logical trade-off is made in terms of the addition and/or modification of product requirements. A 'how much' is established for every 'how' and target/specification values set. The design features interactions are analysed in the 'roof' of the 'house'. Technical comparisons are made against the design requirements, both from the company's existing product and also from the viewpoint of competitive ones under investigation. This could involve some revision of the target value of the design feature.

- Design requirements are then deployed to the next phase in the manufacturing cycle (i.e. product development and detail design – phase 2). Again, any conflicts are prioritized and trade-offs agreed and made.

- The analysis is continued throughout the complete process of manufacture to delivery and even after-sales (i.e. process planning and production planning – phases 3 and 4). In this way, technology restraints are identified and reliability and quality assurance control points identified.

The analysis is progressive and can be stopped at any of the four phases. However, the experience from the Japanese companies is that the greatest benefit is derived when all phases are completed.

A multi-disciplinary team is used to prepare the QFD. The membership of the team is likely to change depending on the stage of QFD being addressed. A number of the seven management tools are also used to assist with the QFD process (e.g. relations diagram, affinity diagram, matrix diagram and systematic diagram).

The following are suggested readings for those wishing to

develop their knowledge of QFD: Akao (1991), Barker (1990) and Eureka and Ryan (1988).

Difficulties associated with QFD are:

- Determining who the customers are and identifying their needs, in particular, when the market is new, customers are not certain of what they want, and knowledge of the market is sketchy. Reconciling the various customer needs at various levels in the supply chain.
- A belief that QFD cannot begin until customer needs have been totally defined.
- Deciding which chart format suits the project under consideration.
- Skipping some of the steps.
- Not addressing fully the issues arising from analysis of the various matrices.
- No internal feedback of the findings.
- Failure to extend QFD past the product planning stage.

Overcome the difficulties by:

- Team-based training on the project being tackled, followed up by regular facilitation by an outside expert.
- A logical system of collecting customer information.
- Adequate analysis undertaken over the complete range of customer needs.
- Paying attention to detail.
- Use of the expertise of team members to overcome any inertia in identifying customer needs and requirements.
- Making full use of relevant data on warranty claims, field failures, previous products and competitive data when developing target specifications.
- Ensuring that the QFD charts are incorporated into the organization's systems and used on an ongoing basis.
- Refining the analysis by discussion with the customer.
- Use of teamwork.

Statistical Process Control

Statistical Process Control is generally accepted to mean management of the process through the use of statistical methods. It has four main uses:

- achieving process stability
- providing guidance on how the process may be improved by the reduction of variation
- Assessing the performance of a process and identifying changes
- Providing information to assist with management decision making

SPC is about control, capability and improvement, but only if used correctly and in an environment conducive to the pursuit of continuous improvement. It is the responsibility of the senior management team to create these conditions. SPC supports the philosophy that products and services can always be improved upon. However, on its own, SPC will not solve problems. A control chart only records the 'voice of the process' and SPC may, at a basic level, simply confirm the presence of a problem. There are many quality management tools and techniques that support and encourage continuous improvement and, in many instances, they should be used both prior to and concurrently with SPC to facilitate analysis and cost cause identification. SPC is basically a measurement technique and it is only when a mechanism is in place to remove and reduce 'special' and 'common' causes of variation that an organization will be using SPC to its fullest potential.

The first step in the use of SPC is to collect data to a plan and plot the gathered data on a graph called a control chart. The control chart is a picture of what is happening in the process at a particular point in time; it is a line graph. The data to be plotted can be in variable or attribute format. Figure 7.6 shows three different types of control charts being employed in a range of situations. Variable data are the result of using some form of measuring system. It is essential to ensure the capability of the measuring system to minimize the potential source of errors that may arise in the data. The measurements may refer to product characteristics (e.g. length) or to process parameters (e.g. temperature). Attribute data are the result of an assessment using go/no-go gauges or pass/fail criteria. It is important to minimize subjectivity when using this pass/fail type of assessment. Reference standards, photographs or illustrations may help and, where possible, the accept/reject characteristics should be agreed with the customer.

The objective of data collection is to get a good overall 'picture' of how a process performs. A data-gathering plan needs to be developed for collection, recording and plotting of data on the

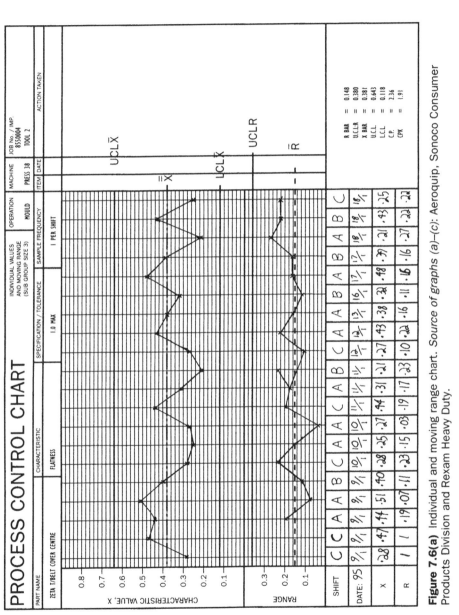

Figure 7.6(a) Individual and moving range chart. *Source of graphs (a)–(c): Aeroquip, Sonoco Consumer Products Division and Rexam Heavy Duty.*

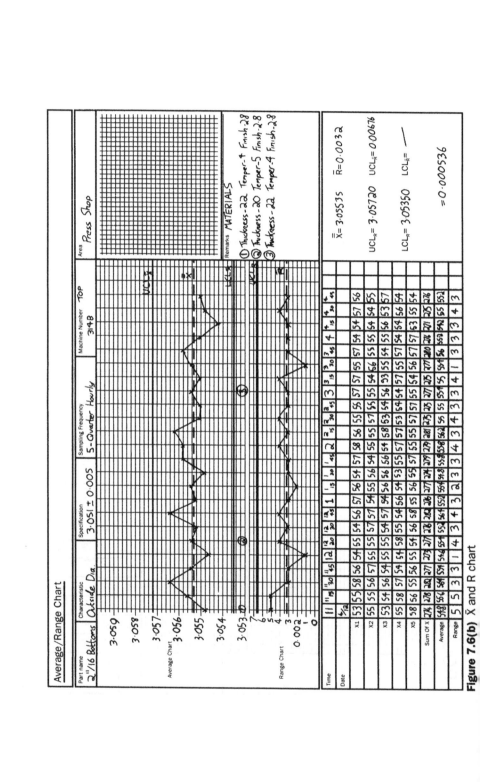

Figure 7.6(b) $\bar{X}$ and R chart

SPCP Chart for Delivery Performance

Plant

Checking frequency: Daily   Team: PL, JN, BK, GA, GH, DC

No. Reason	1	2	3	4	5	6	7	8	9	10	11	12	13	14	15	16	17	18	19	20	21	22	23	24	25	%
P Control Department Mistakes						1	1																			3
Corrl Poor Performance																1										1
Corrl Substandard Work										1																1
Corrl Left in Board Stores											1															1
Corrl Department Mistakes																										1
Sales Incorrect F/O																										
Sales Brought in Items					1																					4
Sales Inserting Urgent Orders																		2								10
European Part Load	2				2										3											18
Despatch Part Load (UK)	2					2	2				1				5	2		1	2	1						18
Despatch Department Mistakes								1																		1
Conversion Waiting For Stereos																										5
Conversion In Board Stores												1		1												
Conversion Dept. Mistakes				1																						1
Maintenance Conversion																										
Maintenance Corrugator								2	1	4	9		3					6								26
M. Control Paper Shortage																										1
M. Control Other Shortage																										
Defect (np)	4	1	0	1	3	3	3	3	1	5	11	2	4	0	11	4	0	1	10	2						69
Sample size (n)	52	52	39	69	76	32	48	75	46	78	52	53	45	23	59	48	28	105	64	45						
% (p)	8	2	0	1	4	9	6	4	2	7	21.4	4	9	0	19	8	0	1	16	4						

UCL

%

UCLp

MEAN

p̄

Figure 7.6(c) p chart for proportion non-conforming

control chart. The data collected should accurately reflect the performance of the process. The factors to be considered are:

- Whether the data are to be collected as variables or attributes.
- The sample or sub-group size.
- The frequency of collection.
- The number of sub-groups to be taken.
- Sampling risks: the risk of a sample indicating that a process is out of control when it is not, and, on the other hand, the risk of the sample failing to detect that a process is out of control.
- Costs: the cost of taking the sample, the cost of investigation and correction of special causes, and the cost of non-conforming output

Different data gathering plans may give different pictures of a process and there are many economic models of control charts. However, consideration of statistical criteria and practical experience have led to the formulation of general guidelines for sample size and intervals between samples. For example, in the automotive-related industry they have led to the widespread acceptance (for variables) of a sample size of five, a one-hourly sampling frequency, the taking of between twenty and thirty sub-groups as a test for the stability of a process, and the use of three standard error control limits. To obtain a meaningful picture of process performance from attributes data, and to ensure that the statistical theory supporting the design of the control chart is valid, larger samples (i.e. greater than twenty-five) are required.

Control charts using mean and range are the most popular variables charts in use and they are now used to outline the methods of control chart construction. There are four major steps:

- Calculate each sub-group average ($\bar{x}$) and range value (R). These data are plotted on the chart.
- Calculate the process average ($\bar{\bar{X}}$) and process mean range ($\bar{R}$). These statistics are plotted on the chart as heavy broken lines.
- Calculate and plot on the chart the control limits. These control limits are drawn on the chart as solid lines and are set at three standard errors or $A_2\bar{R}$ from the reference value.
- Analyse and interpret the control charts for special and common causes of variation.

The process average, $\bar{\bar{X}}$, is the mean of all the sample means, and the mean range, $\bar{R}$, is the average of all the sample ranges. These are used to calculate control limits and are drawn on the chart as a guide for analysis. They reflect the natural variability of the process and are calculated using constants, appropriate to the sample size, which are taken from statistical tables. The formulae used are:

Mean control chart:

Upper control limit (UCL$\bar{x}$) = $\bar{\bar{X}} + A_2\bar{R}$

Lower control limit (LCL$\bar{x}$) = $\bar{\bar{X}} - A_2\bar{R}$

where A_2 is a constant derived from statistical tables and is dependent upon the sample size.

Range control chart:

Upper control limit (UCL$_R$) = $D_4\bar{R}$

Lower control limit (LCL$_R$) = $D_3\bar{R}$

where D_4 and D_3 are constants derived from statistical tables and are dependent upon the sample size.

The range and mean charts are analysed separately, but the patterns of variation occurring in the two charts are compared with each other to assist in identifying special causes that may be affecting the process. The range chart monitors uniformity and the mean chart focuses on where the process is centred.

Special causes of variation influence some or all of the measurements in different ways. They occur intermittently and reveal themselves as unusual patterns of variation on a control chart. They should be identified and rectified, and with improved process and/or product design, their occurrence should, in the long term, be minimized. They include:

- change in raw material
- change in machine setting
- broken tool, die or pattern
- failure to clean equipment
- equipment malfunction
- keying in incorrect data

Indications of special causes are:

- A data point falling outside the control limits.
- A run of points in a particular direction, consistently increasing or decreasing. In general, a run of seven consecutive points is used as the guide.
- A run of points all on one side of the reference value $\bar{\bar{X}}$ or $\bar{R}$. In general, a run of seven consecutive points is used as the guide.
- Substantially more or less than two-thirds of the points plotted lying within the mid-third section of the chart. This might indicate that the control limits or plot points have been miscalculated or misplotted, or that data have been edited in some way, or that process or the sampling method are stratified.
- Any other obvious non-random patterns.

Common causes influence all measurements in the same way. They produce the natural pattern of variation observed in data when they are free of special causes. Common causes arise from many sources and do not reveal themselves as unique patterns of deviation; consequently, they are often difficult to identify. If only common-cause variation is present the process is considered to be stable, and therefore predictable. Typical common causes include:

- badly maintained machines
- poor lighting
- poor workstation layout
- poor instructions
- poor supervision
- materials and equipment not suited to the requirements

An argument in favour of inspection by attributes is that it is not such a time consuming task as that for variables, so the sample size can be much larger. It is also less costly to undertake. Experience shows that attribute data often exists in a variety of forms in an organization, although it may not necessarily be analysed statistically. A variety of charts can be used to organise attribute data in order to assist with process control. The choice of chart is dependent on whether the sample size is kept constant and whether the inspection criterion is a non-conforming item or a non-conformity within an item. The main types of attributes chart for non-conforming items are proportion/percentage (p) and number defective (np) charts; while for non-conformities they are proportion (u) and number (c) charts.

The collection and organizing of data is almost identical to that described for variables, except that for each sample, the number (or proportion or percentage) of non-conforming items or non-conformities is recorded and plotted. The reference value on attribute charts is the process average. The control limits are again three standard errors from the process average.

Process capability

Because it is easier to understand, the capability of processes using attribute data is discussed first.

With the np chart (number of non-conforming items), it is usual to express the average number of acceptable items per sample as a percentage to quantify capability:

$$\left(1 - \frac{n\bar{p}}{n}\right) \times 100\%$$

With the p chart, it is simply the average proportion of acceptable items expressed as a percentage:

$$(1 - \bar{p}) \times 100\%$$

With measured data, the use of indices such as Cpk and Cp has been in increasing use. The capability of a process is defined as three standard deviations on either side of the process average when the process is normally distributed. The Cp index is found as the result of comparing the perceived spread of the process with the specification width or tolerance band.

$$Cp = \frac{\text{Total specified tolerance}}{\text{Process spread}}$$

As the Cp index compares the 'spread of the process' with the tolerance band, it is primarily concerned with precision. It is for this reason that Cp is often defined as 'process potential'.

The Cpk index takes into account both accuracy and precision by incorporating them into the calculations. Because it assesses both accuracy and precision, they are often defined as 'process capability' measures. There are two formulae:

$$Cpk = \frac{USL - \bar{\bar{X}}}{\text{Three standard deviations}}$$

where USL is the upper specification limit and $\bar{\bar{X}}$ is the process average, and:

$$Cpk = \frac{\bar{\bar{X}} - LSL}{\text{Thee standard deviations}}$$

where LSL is the lower specification limit.

It is customary to quote the smaller of the two values, giving the more critical part of the measurements distribution.

The comments made on capability relate to data collected over the long term from a stable, in-control and predictable process. Often short-term capability needs to be investigated particularly for new products or processes and as part of a supplier verification programme. In this case the time scale is then reduced to cover only a few hours run of the process. The data are collected in the same manner as for the initial control chart study, but the frequency of sampling is increased to get as many samples (of size n) as possible to give a good picture of the process (i.e. about twenty samples of size n). Data is plotted on the control chart with appropriate limits, but the following indices are calculated: Pp, the preliminary process potential, and Ppk, = the preliminary process capability. The formulae are exactly as for Cp and Cpk but the minimum requirements may be higher.

All capability indices are estimates derived from estimates of the process variation. The reliability or confidence in the estimate of the process standard deviation is a function of:

- The amount of data that has been collected.
- The manner in which the data was collected.
- The capability of the measuring system (i.e. its accuracy and precision).
- The skill of the people using the measuring system.
- People's knowledge and understanding of statistics.

Further details on SPC are provided by Montgomery (1991), Oakland (1997), Owen (1989) and Price (1984).

The typical difficulties encountered in the introduction and application of SPC are:

- Poor understanding and awareness within the company of the purpose of SPC.
- Ill-defined purpose of use.
- Perception that the charting of data is time consuming.
- Lack of knowledge/expertise of SPC, including when to employ it, which charts to use, and uncertainty about control chart design.
- Inappropriate product characteristic and process parameters measured.
- Lack of action from senior management.
- Inadequate training of those who will be involved in its use and application.
- Lack of support in analysing the data.
- Confusion between control and capability.
- Understanding the difference between control limits and specification.
- Applying SPC to a particular process.
- Inadequate attention to training issues such as timing, design, skills of trainers and follow-up audit of the skills taught.
- Operating personnel not being made responsible for the measurement and plotting of data on the control chart.
- Inadequate information on the control chart and process log.
- Insufficient attention to the control of variation within the measurement methods and equipment.
- Using SPC software before the logic underpinning SPC is understood.

The majority of difficulties are caused by the lack of commitment, awareness, understanding, involvement and leadership of middle and senior managers. While SPC may be seen to be a bottom-up activity, used by people responsible for controlling a process, it needs management to take their obligations for continuous improvement seriously if it is to be effective over the longer term. It should not be treated merely as a source of control charts, which management use to present to their customers a picture suggesting they are doing something positive about improvement, but as a technique to produce improved quality more economically.

Overcome the difficulties by:

- Defining the purpose of the control chart.
- Involving operating staff at all stages.

- Stating the aims of the chart clearly.
- Defining the data measurement criteria.
- Defining how the data is to be collected and by whom.
- Constantly asking whether data collection is adding value to the process.
- Ensuring that expert support is available during data collection, analysis and interpretation.
- Ensuring that procedures are in place to cover the changes that result from the charting exercise.
- Defining terminology and adhere to it.
- Ensuring that the objectives and reasons for the use of SPC are clearly communicated throughout the organization.
- Management being good role models and using SPC in their own decision making.
- Putting reaction, discipline and corrective procedures in place to respond to the plotted data and/or out-of-control conditions.
- Challenging the validity of the data that has been recorded and asking how it can be used to improve the process.

Summary

The concepts and methods underlying techniques are, in the main, more complex than those associated with tools. They are, in general, more likely to be used by technical specialists whereas tools are generally the province of staff from the operating level of the business. This is reflected in the wide range of difficulties encountered with their use and application. A major thread running through the difficulties is related to knowledge, understanding and the ability and confidence to use the technique. Unlike tools, with a number of the techniques there is sometimes no correct way of constructing them, and some form of experimentation and assessment of results is required. A case in point is SPC. Most people claim to understand the fundamentals of SPC but there are not so many who have the ability to think through how it can be applied to processes outside the normal five parts every hour from metal production processes. There is also a shortage of expertise in diagnosing mistakes made with control chart design and process capability calculations, in particular when the measurements are linked to SPC software.

For each technique described, ways of overcoming the difficulties have been explored. The common issues to which attention needs to be paid include: appropriate education and training by those knowledgeable about the technique(s) being taught, senior management support and commitment to encourage the use of the technique, the use of teamwork in constructing and deploying the techniques, and audit and assessment of their use, including making appropriate changes to improve their effectiveness.

8 Tools and Techniques: An Assessment Methodology

Introduction

In the preceding chapters a wide-ranging discussion of tools and techniques has taken place, including practical applications, the conditions and platforms needed for them to be used effectively and the issues and difficulties that can arise from use, and indeed, misuse. This final chapter provides the means, in the form of an audit methodology, for identifying the potential difficulties that impinge on the effective use of tools and techniques in an organization. But before going into details of the methodology it is worth summarizing what is meant by a tool and technique.

Tools and techniques are practical methods, skills or means that are applied to particular tasks. They come in many different forms and levels of complexity; for example, a simple cartoon picture is a tool used to convey a message, story or piece of information, whereas risk analysis is a complex statistical engineering technique applied during the product development process. Thus, a tool may be described as any device with a clearly defined application; it is often narrow in focus and used on its own. Other examples of tools are cause and effect diagrams, run charts, diagrams, histograms etc. A technique, on the other hand, is something with a wider application than a tool. It usually requires more conceptual thought and skill to use it effectively. It may even be viewed as a collection of tools. For example, statistical process control is a technique that employs a variety of charts, graphs and analysis methods, all of which are necessary for its effective use.

As outlined earlier, there are many influences, both internal and external to the organization, which impact on the successful use and application of tools and techniques. For example, appropriate training, adequate post-training support and coaching, use within a structured problem-solving approach, a perceived need for the tool and technique being applied and the effective use of a tool and technique by an individual or team need to be recognized, communicated and celebrated. In chapter 4 these various influences were categorized as experience, management, resources, education and training, and they featured strongly in the development of the audit methodology.

The methodology consists of:

1 Assessment grid
2 Questionnaire
3 Semi-structured interviews
4 Observation of tools and techniques in practice

The fourth point is recommended to support the three more formal methods. Organizations, departments and their workforces can be adept at camouflage in order to portray what they think are the 'right answers' and to present a 'rosy picture' to those involved in evaluating the use of tools and techniques. Observation by a person knowledgeable in tools and techniques can soon establish the actual situation.

These approaches can be used separately as well as in combinations. Much depends on the organization's objectives for the exercise. For example, the use of the assessment grid and questionnaire in combination will provide an evaluation within a department or across the organization, depending on the scale of the analysis, of employees' awareness of tools and techniques, and their usage, and will pinpoint the areas of difficulties, as individuals perceive them. The information supplied by this can provide the focus for more in-depth probing using semi-structured interviews. The assessment grid can be first used on its own to undertake a 'health check' of potential areas for concern. This can be followed by more in-depth analysis using the questionnaire and/or semi-structured interviews. In this way the data provided by the questionnaire and interviews helps to interpret the analysis of the assessment grid and further explore the applicability of the tools and techniques. For example:

1 Why is only one particular tool or technique used by a department?
2 Why are the tools and techniques that are recognized not being used?
3 If a tool is being used, is it fully understood and being used correctly?

The objectives of the assessment methodology, include:

- Establishing the success or otherwise of the use of tools and techniques as perceived by the user.
- Identifying barriers to the implementation of tools and techniques.
- Identifying differences in the awareness, use and perceived utility of the tools and techniques.
- Highlighting the degree of formality of use.
- Identifying which tools and techniques are used by each department and pinpointing the scale of usage.
- Pinpointing training needs.
- Establishing the difficulties arising due to training.
- Pinpointing areas that need more management commitment and support.
- Assessing available supporting mechanism (e.g. people, equipment).
- Identifying misuse.
- Pinpointing gaps between recognition and use.
- Assessing whether the use and application of tools and techniques is fully appreciated and whether their objectives and role are fully understood.
- Examining the uses to which the tool or technique is put.
- Identifying further scope for the tools and techniques that are currently in use.
- Highlighting those tools and techniques that need greater usage in order to increase departmental and/or company efficiency.
- Helping to raise the profile of the tools and techniques in common use.
- Assessing whether the culture of the organization encourages the use of tools and techniques.

The strength of the methodology is its flexibility, since it provides a framework for establishing not only the negative aspects affecting tools and techniques, but also for highlighting the positive aspects. This is equally important, since establishing the factors that make for effective use and application of tools and techniques in one area of the organization can facilitate their transfer to others, thereby building on best practice. The assessment can also provide a key input, in particular, to the processes and resources criteria, of the self-assessment undertaken using the European Foundation for Quality Management or Malcolm Baldrige National Quality Award Models for Business Excellence.

Assessment Grid

The Recognition and Use grid is given in figure 8.1a and the Application grid in figure 8.1b. These grids need to be supported by a sketch of each tool and technique, using company-specific examples. This helps to get over any confusion regarding the title and content of each tool and technique and its description and terminology.

A plan must be developed on how the assessment grid is to be used. Initial decisions need to be made as to whether it will be used company-wide or restricted to a sample of departments and if the latter which of the departments and functions are to be investigated. The number of people who are to complete the Assessment grid needs to be decided. If the number of staff employed in a department that is to be examined is small then everybody should complete the grid. On the other hand, if the department or function involves a large number of staff then an appropriate sample needs to be selected to provide an indication of usage and an illustration of trends at each level of the organizational hierarchy. It is recommended that the sample selected should include senior, middle and first-line managers, staff and operators, employees involved in improvement teams and employees not involved in improvement teams. Decisions also need to be made with respect to how the data is to be analysed (e.g. department by department, function by function, management and support staff compared to plant personnel).

In the first place the Recognition and Use grid should be completed by all people taking part in the assessment. They should indicate with a tick the tools and techniques they recognize on the grid. This recognition relates to the name only of the tool or technique, without people necessarily understanding how to construct it or how to apply the tool or technique in practice. Once this has

Please indicate on the grid ONLY the techniques and tools you recognize. For those that you have recognized, if you use them for **any** purpose, not only for quality-related matters, please tick the box marked use.

Example	Recognize	Use
Seven basic tools		
Cause and effect	✔	
Check sheet/concentration diagrams		
Control charts		
Graphs/charts	✔	✔
Histograms	✔	✔
Pareto analysis	✔	✔
Scatter diagrams	✔	

	Recognize	Use
Seven basic tools		
Cause and effect		
Check sheet/concentration diagrams		
Control charts		
Graphs/charts		
Histograms		
Pareto analysis		
Scatter diagrams		
Seven management tools		
Affinity diagrams		
Arrow diagrams/critical path analysis		
Matrix data analysis methods		
Matrix diagrams		
Process decision programme chart (PDPC)		
Relation diagrams		
Systematic diagrams/tree diagrams		
Techniques		
Benchmarking		
Brainstorming/brainwriting		
Departmental purpose analysis (DPA)		
Design of experiments (Taguchi, DOE)		
Failure mode and effects analysis (FMEA)		
Flow charts		
Force field analysis		
Problem solving methodology		
Quality costs		
Quality function deployment (QFD)		
Questionnaire		
Sampling		
Statistical process control (SPC)		
*		
*		
*		
*		
*		

* Add any company–specific techniques and tools not indicated on the list

Please complete the grid ONLY for the techniques or tools you indicated on the recognition and use grid. Do not attempt to fill it in its entirety. They may be occasions when some of the categories cannot be allocated a score; in that case insert 9 (not applicable)

Score out of 5 in each of the categories where:

1 = No value

2 = Low value (e.g. little used, not understood, little or poor training, etc.)

3 = Some value (e.g. basic understanding, small benefits, basic training, etc.)

4 = High value (e.g. good understanding, some benefits, reasonable training, etc.)

5 = Very high value (e.g. complete understanding, excellent benefits, effective traing, etc.)

9 = Not applicable or no training

	Importance 5	Relevance 4	Use 2	Understand 3	Application 3	Resources 2	Management 1	Training 1	Benefit 4
For example: *Pareto analysis*	Importance	Relevance	Use	Understand	Application	Resources	Management	Training	Benefit
Seven basic tools									
Cause and effect									
Check sheet/concentration diagrams									
Control charts									
Graphs/charts									
Histograms									
Pareto analysis									
Scatter diagrams									
Seven management tools									
Affinity diagrams									
Arrow diagrams/critical path analysis									
Matrix data analysis methods									
Matrix diagrams									
Process decision programme chart (PDPC)									
Relation diagrams									
Systematic diagrams/tree diagrams									
Techniques									
Benchmarking									
Brainstorming/brainwriting									
Departmental purpose analysis (DPA)									
Design of experiments (Taguchi, DOE)									
Failure mode and effects analysis (FMEA)									
Flow charts									
Force field analysis									
Problem solving methodology									
Quality costs									
Quality function deployment (QFD)									
Questionnaire									
Sampling									
Statistical process control (SPC)									
Other techniques, tools, systems									
For example:									
ISO 9000 series									
Quality operating system QS 9000									
Other awards (e.g. EQA)									

b

Figure 8.1 (a) Recognition and Use grid and (b) Application grid

been done the next step is to indicate with a tick which of the tools and techniques that have been recognized are actually used. The Application grid should then be completed for the techniques and tools that have been indicated as being used by the participants in the Recognition and Use grid. The following are the categories that are assessed in the Application grid (see figure 8.1b):

- Importance to you in your job.
- Relevance to your job.
- How much you use it in your job.
- Your understanding of the technique or tool.
- The degree to which you can apply it to your job.
- Availability of resources (i.e. money, people, technology, facilities, equipment and time) necessary to apply the technique or tool.
- Organization and management. The degree to which your manager and organization are committed to the use of tools and techniques, shown by their support and encouragement and their willingness to act on the results.
- Training. The effectiveness of the training you received with regard to content, being able to apply the technique or tool to your job or task, the method of delivery, time between training and using the technique or tool.
- Benefits. Whether you regard the tool or technique as being of benefit to you in doing your job.

A score out of five should be attributed to each of the nine categories, using the scoring system outlined below as guidance:

- 1 = No value
- 2 = Low value (i.e. little used, not understood, little or poor training etc.)
- 3 = Some value (i.e. basic understanding, small benefits, basic training etc.)
- 4 = High value (i.e. good understanding, some benefits, reasonable training etc.)
- 5 = Very high value (i.e. complete understanding, excellent benefits, effective training etc.)

Where there has been no training or it is not appropriate to attribute a value, a score of 9 should be used.

There is no need to complete the Application grid in its entirety;

there may be occasions when some of the categories for an individual tool or technique cannot be allocated a score.

In analysing the data from the Application grid, the information on resources, organization and management, and training can be used as the starting point to determine the degree of difficulty, whilst that on benefits, relevance and importance can be treated as an indication of those tools and techniques that are useful to the organization.

The data obtained can be analysed and presented in a number of ways using statistical analysis such as SPSS, spreadsheets, graphs and tables. In this manner the data can be manipulated and trends identified, in particular, to identify the importance and relevance of each tool and technique. Figures 8.2 to 8.5 show some typical presentation methods of the analysis.

Questionnaire

The questionnaire is given in appendix A. The first section of the questionnaire is designed to obtain quantitative data about job profiles and organizational structure. It includes attitudinal questions on the use and application of tools and techniques. The

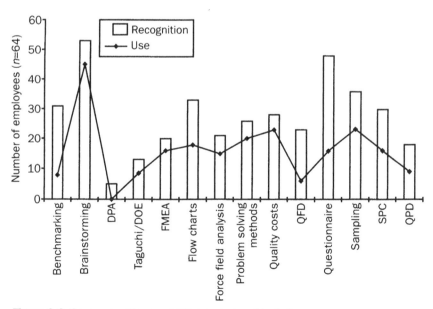

Figure 8.2 Company-wide recognition and use of techniques

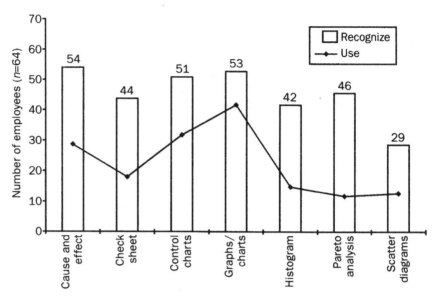

Figure 8.3 Company-wide recognition and use of the seven basic quality control tools

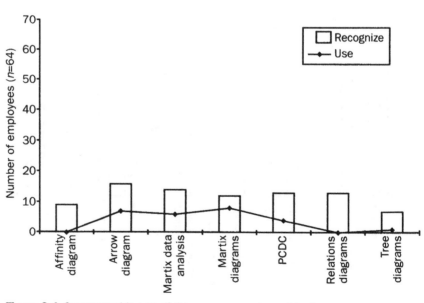

Figure 8.4 Company-wide use of the seven management tools

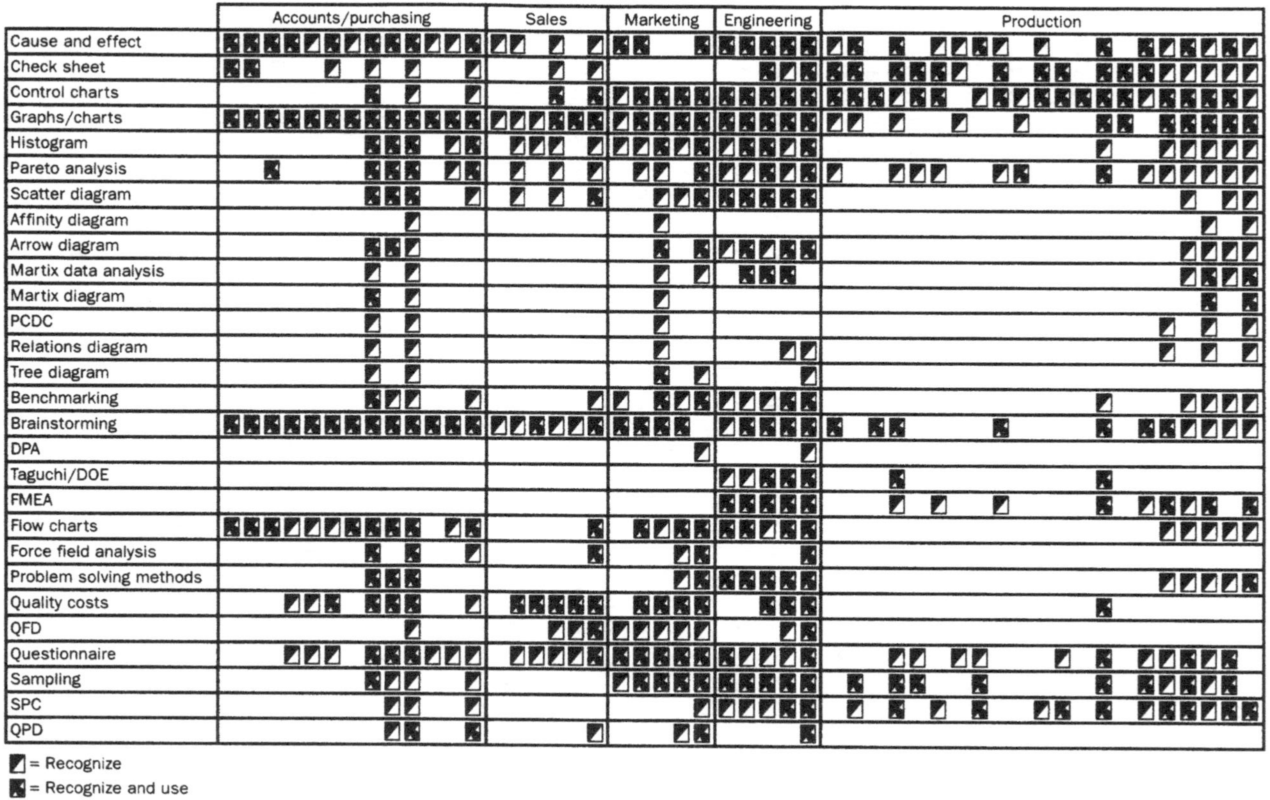
Accounts/purchasing
Sales
Marketing
Engineering
Production
Cause and effect
Check sheet
Control charts
Graphs/charts
Histogram
Pareto analysis
Scatter diagram
Affinity diagram
Arrow diagram
Martix data analysis
Martix diagram
PCDC
Relations diagram
Tree diagram
Benchmarking
Brainstorming
DPA
Taguchi/DOE
FMEA
Flow charts
Force field analysis
Problem solving methods
Quality costs
QFD
Questionnaire
Sampling
SPC
QPD
= Recognize
= Recognize and use

Figure 8.5 Recognition and use pattern analysis

simple format enables the reviewer to obtain the necessary information, which provides the background for analysis and interpretation of the data that is gathered.

Semi-Structured Interviews

The questions outlined in appendix B should be used as the basis for conducting a series of semi-structured interviews. The interviews should last for approximately one hour, and be conducted with between ten and twenty people, depending on the size of the department and organization being analysed. Random selection of those to be interviewed is the preferred means but this is not always practical. If the assessment is being conducted on a company-wide basis, it is essential that individuals are selected from a cross-section of the organizational hierarchy and across all functions. Each person who is to be interviewed should be informed of the purpose of the interview at least one week prior to it taking place, with emphasis being placed on the fact that the investigation is fact finding and not a finger pointing or blame exercise. Interviewees should be encouraged to seek the views of others in their own working area in relation to the influences that exert an effect on the successful use and application of tools and techniques.

Using the guidelines provided in appendix B, the interviews should explore the issues and difficulties that arise as a result of the exertion of company-specific influences on: the role of the technique or tool in the improvement process, organization and infrastructure of the company, data collection, and use and application of the tool or technique. Some of the issues can be explored in greater or less detail, depending on the person being interviewed, the job, position within the organization and experience. Discussion of the issues and difficulties identified will pinpoint the areas for improvement. A small number of questions are given as examples for the five influencing categories. Questions can be developed and tailored to suit the organization under examination, and the person being interviewed.

Although the main thrust of the investigation centres on issues and difficulties that affect the use and application of tools and techniques, those highlighted often impinge on other areas of operations management and organizational behaviour.

Summary

The purpose of this chapter was to provide the means by which the use and application of tools and techniques can be assessed within an organization. The methodology described will help the organization to identify gaps between (1) perceived importance and relevance, (2) benefits and usage, and (3) application and training. It will also provide the basis for a diagnostic analysis along lines such as:

> 'There is little management commitment to using tools and techniques and virtually no training.'

> 'Tools and techniques are perceived as important and relevant by personnel from Department x but a lack of training and management support are inhibiting their use.'

> 'Department x recognizes and use more tools and techniques than department y. This is explained by the fact that . . .'

Running through the book are a number of common themes which support and aid the effective use of tools and techniques, regardless of their complexity. The use of the assessment methodology will highlight these themes. Therefore, in bringing the book to a close it is useful to summarize these themes. They include:

- Providing a good explanation as to why individual tools and techniques are being used.
- Providing guidance to employees as to which tool and technique they should be using and for what purpose. To aid this, a matrix should be developed relating each tool and technique to its main application and use,
- Understanding the limitations of how and when tools and techniques can best be used.
- There are a number of reasons why companies use tools and techniques; for example, customer contractual requirements, considering them as a panacea to solve a particular problem, and as part of the introduction and development of TQM. It should be recognized that the reasons for use will have a key influence on how the tool or technique will be perceived within the company.
- A planned approach for the application of tools and techniques is necessary. The temptation to single out one tool or technique for special attention should be resisted, and to get maximum

benefit from the use of tools and techniques they should be used in combination.

- Using qualified trainers to introduce employees to tools and techniques and ensuring that these trainees transfer their knowledge to employees in the workplace.
- Using the tools and techniques to develop team members in their problem solving knowledge and skills.
- Wherever possible, delegating tasks for the use of the tool or technique to team members to encourage involvement and participation.
- Only using tools and techniques when the need has been identified. Do not let them overtake the original problem solving purpose or delay the results. However, their application should be encouraged as part of daily work activities.
- At operative and first-line supervisor level, tools and techniques are likely to be seen by perceived as a means of measuring their performance and consequently they may not be given the attention they deserve. The need to use tools and techniques can also be seen by these staff as obstacles to their meeting production schedules. These issues need to be considered in implementation and training plans.
- Using the tools and techniques to sell improvement ideas to management.
- The tools and techniques should be used to facilitate improvement and integrated into the way the business works, rather than being used and viewed as 'bolt-on' techniques.
- The way the tool or technique is applied and how its results are interpreted are critical to its successful use; a tool or technique is only as good as the person who is using it.
- Tools and techniques on their own are not enough; they need an environment that is conducive to improvement and to their use. An organization's senior mangers have a key role to play in the effective use of tools and techniques.

Appendix A: Questionnaire

This section asks questions about your job, your attitude and your understanding of improvement concepts before examining more specifically the use and application of tools and techniques. Some questions require a tick only; others ask for your comments.

Please attempt to answer all of the questions, in particular those that ask for your comments. These are extremely valuable and will aid the analysis. If you are unable to answer a question because you do not hold the relevant information, or it is not applicable, indicate 'Don't know' or 'Not applicable'.

SECTION 1

1. General information

1.1 State the length of time you have been with company.

_____ years/months

1.2 Has the team/function undergone reorganization (i.e. in the last five years)?

Yes ☐
No ☐
Don't know ☐

1.3 Has reorganization affected morale within the team/function?

Low morale				High morale	
1	2	3	4	5	
☐	☐	☐	☐	☐	Don't know ☐

2. Your Job

2.1 What function do you work in?

_____

_____

_____

2.2 Please describe briefly what your function, section or department does.

_____

_____

_____

_____

_____

2.3 What is your job within your section, function or department (e.g. operator, supervisor, manager, secretary)?

_____

_____

_____

2.4 Do you have any other responsibilities, including projects directly or indirectly related to your job?

Yes ☐
No ☐

If Yes, please give details.

_____

_____

_____

_____

_____

2.5 To whom do you report?

Team leader ☐
Supervisor ☐
Section leader/manager ☐
Functional/departmental manager ☐
Managing director, chief executive
    officer or other senior manager,
    please specify ☐

2.6 Are you ever required to move between sections, functions or departments?

Frequently ☐
Occasionally ☐
Seldom ☐
Never ☐

2.7 Have you been directly involved in any improvement activities not directly related to your normal working routine (e.g. quality facilitator, quality team member)?

Yes ☐
No ☐

If Yes, please give details.

_____

_____

_____

3. Interaction and communication

3.1 In your opinion is there sufficient communication between your function/department and related sections or departments?

Good communication with all other sections/departments ☐
Good communication with most other sections/departments ☐
Good communication with some sections/departments ☐
Sufficient only to carry out duties ☐
Little or no communication between sections ☐

3.2 In what way, do you think, could communication between sections or departments could be improved?

_____

_____

_____

_____

3.3 Quality-related communications within the organization: to what extent do you agree with the following statements?

	Agree	Tend to agree	Neither agree nor disagree	Tend to disagree	Disagree
You are well informed on quality matters	☐	☐	☐	☐	☐
You receive regular communications on quality matters	☐	☐	☐	☐	☐
The information you receive does not reflect what is going on	☐	☐	☐	☐	☐
You have no idea about the organization's quality policies	☐	☐	☐	☐	☐

3.4 How are they communicated?

_____

_____

_____

4. Tools and techniques

4.1 Are tools and techniques used in your department (e.g. SPC, Pareto analysis, cause and effect, control charts etc.)?

Yes ☐
No ☐
Don't know ☐

4.2 How long have tools and techniques been used in your section/department

Less than 6 months ☐
6–12 months ☐
1–2 years ☐
2–5 years ☐
More than 5 years ☐
Don't know ☐

4.3 Why are tools and techniques used in your section, function or department (more than one may be selected)?

Problem solving ☐   Data collection ☐
Process maintenance ☐   Data presentation ☐
Product quality ☐   Setting priorities ☐
Problem prevention ☐   Other (please specify)
Continuous improvement ☐
Customer requirement ☐   _____ ☐
Cannot say ☐

4.4 How long have *you* been using tools and techniques in your job?

Less than 6 months ☐
6–12 months ☐
1–2 years ☐
2–5 years ☐
More than 5 years ☐

4.5 Have you used tools and techniques for any other purpose/project not directly relating to your normal job?

Yes ☐
No ☐

If Yes, in what capacity?

_____

_____

_____

4.6 To your knowledge was there any resistance to the introduction of tools and techniques in your section, function or department?

_____

_____

_____

4.7 To what extent do you agree with the following statements?

	Agree	Tend to agree	Neither agree nor disagree	Tend to disagree	Disagree
Resistance to the introduction oftools and techniques was due to changes in work practices	☐	☐	☐	☐	☐
People were unable to recognize the benefits	☐	☐	☐	☐	☐
Insufficient understanding	☐	☐	☐	☐	☐
Lack of experience	☐	☐	☐	☐	☐

4.8 To what extent do you agree with the following statements with regard to tools and techniques used in your job, section, function or department?

	Agree	Tend to agree	Neither agree nor disagree	Tend to disagree	Disagree
They do not suit the process	☐	☐	☐	☐	☐
They are not sufficiently understood by personnel	☐	☐	☐	☐	☐
Managers/supervisors do not support their use	☐	☐	☐	☐	☐
There is little point in using them as no action will be taken	☐	☐	☐	☐	☐
The results may be used adversely against the operator	☐	☐	☐	☐	☐
There is no benefit to be gained in their use	☐	☐	☐	☐	☐

4.9 Do _you_ use tools and techniques as part of your daily working activities?

Yes ☐

No ☐

If Yes, please give a recent example.

_____

_____

_____

_____

_____

4.10 To what extent do you agree with the following statements in relation to the application of tools and techniques to processes/procedures associated with *your* job, section, function or department?

	Agree	Tend to agree	Neither agree nor disagree	Tend to disagree	Disagree
They are a waste of time; no one acts on the results	☐	☐	☐	☐	☐
They are essential to manage my job effectively	☐	☐	☐	☐	☐
Some are more useful than others	☐	☐	☐	☐	☐
They do not produce meaningful results	☐	☐	☐	☐	☐
They produce too much information to analyse satisfactory	☐	☐	☐	☐	☐

4.11 Do you find the use of tools and techniques useful?

Frequently ☐
Occasionally ☐
Seldom ☐
Never ☐

5. Continuous Improvement, Problem solving, Special projects

5.1 Have you been involved in the decision making process to select areas for improvement?

Yes ☐
No ☐

If Yes, please give details.

_____

_____

_____

5.2 Given the opportunity, would you like to be involved in an improvement project?

Yes ☐
Occasionally ☐
No ☐

5.3 Is there a person (quality facilitator or technique expert) available to assist in the application of tools and techniques in your section, function or department?

Yes ☐
No ☐
Don't know ☐

5.4 With regard to the quality facilitators who are known to you, to what extent do you agree with the following statements?

	Agree	Tend to agree	Neither agree nor disagree	Tend to disagree	Disagree
They have sufficient understanding of the processes in your section or department	☐	☐	☐	☐	☐
They have little understanding of the product of your section or department	☐	☐	☐	☐	☐
They are knowledgeable about tools and techniques	☐	☐	☐	☐	☐
They can help apply tools and techniques successfully to your processes	☐	☐	☐	☐	☐
They have sufficient authority to ensure quality tasks are carried out	☐	☐	☐	☐	☐
They have credibility with the members of your section/function	☐	☐	☐	☐	☐
They have credibility with the managers of your section, function or department	☐	☐	☐	☐	☐

Appendix B: The Framework for Semi-Structured Interviews

Personal Profile

Organizations, regardless of their size and complexity, are composed of people. It is people who use tools and techniques and they are also subject to many of the influences associated with tools and techniques. Consequently, the starting point in probing the use and application of tools and techniques should be with the individual.

Typical areas to be addressed are:
- Personal profile:
  - age, length of service
  - type of job, length of time in the current department, function or area
  - general background
  - what steps have they followed to get to their present position?
- Individual's view of the organization
  - what do they think of the organization?
  - does any other member of their family work for the company?
  - do they see their current position as a step in a long term career plan (if appropriate) or do they think they will remain with the company until retirement?
- The individual's view of TQM:
  - what does TQM mean to them?
  - how has it affected their job?
  - what do they do now that is different from before?
- Tools and techniques: at the early stages of the interview detailed information is not required, but it is important to get a 'flavour' of the individual's knowledge of tools and techniques. This then sets the pattern for more detailed questions. With some members of the organization it may be appropriate to provide pictorial examples of tools and techniques, as a memory aid.
  - do they recognize a selection of tools and techniques?
  - do they use them in their job as part of the daily routine or for specialist purposes such as project work or in improvement team activities?
  - if they are new to the organization have they used tools and techniques in their previous organization?

If there is a negative response to the questions (i.e. the individual fails to recognize or acknowledge tools and techniques) then there are two routes to follow. The first is to establish how long they have been with the organization and the length of time in that particular job. It may be the case that they have yet to receive any training in tools and techniques. If this is the case the interview may be terminated. For those individuals who respond positively to the questions and those who appear to be resistant or dismissive of TQM and tools and techniques, then the next stage is to gain more detailed information.

Organization and Local Culture

It is essential when investigating the specific issues of tools and techniques that the broader cultural aspects are not ignored. This is particularly important for organizations that have multiple locations and that wish to transpose company quality policies into each of their business units. What works well in one location may not be successful in another, both within a country and from country to country.

Typical questions are:

- Are you, or have you even been, involved in any company improvement initiative?
- Would you like to become involved?
- Have you ever suggested areas for improvement?
- Where do you consider that the responsibility for quality assurance and continuous improvement lies?
- Who should take responsibility for the processes and procedures used in your department?

Issues and Difficulties

The following questions are intended to find out more details relating to the individual's opinions and knowledge of the use, application, issues and difficulties associated with tools and techniques. The questions are grouped under the categories of Experience, Management, Resources, Education and Training. Where appropriate the questions are focused toward their impact on the organization and infrastructure, the role of the technique or tool, data collection, and use and application. It must be remembered when interpreting interviewees' responses, that they are opinions and are entirely subjective; therefore, they should not be viewed in isolation.

Experience

The length of time an organization has been following a TQM initiative and its subsequent use of tools and techniques reflects on their application to different situations and functions. Therefore it is important to establish the current health of the initiative.

Typical questions include:

- How long has the organization been following an improvement initiative? Has there been more than one?
- Are the initiatives followed through?
- Do you consider that the initiatives have been successful?
- Are there conflicting strategies between quality and other functions or policies of the organization?
- What do you consider to be the main difficulties being experienced with continuous improvement.

What are tools and techniques?   Very often there is confusion over what constitutes a tool and technique, and what is a management tool. Individuals may use presentation tools, data gathering techniques or statistical methods without the realization they actually fall into the category of tools and techniques. In these circumstances it is essential to establish if any tools and techniques are used and in what circumstances. This then aids further discussion on the specific difficulties of tools and techniques.

Typical questions are:

- Do you use graphs, charts or statistical analysis as part of your normal daily activities? If yes, to what purpose?
- Do you consider them to be tools and techniques?

More detailed questions then follow with regard to continuous improvement, problem solving, project work and teamwork.

- Are you encouraged to use tools and techniques?
- Is there someone in your department who encourages and champions their use?
- Does anyone check to see if and how you are using tools and techniques?

- Is there a facilitator or anyone else to provide aid and support when you are required to apply a particular tool or technique?
- Have you used or considered using some of the more complex techniques such as design of experiments or quality function deployment?
- Is there a potential for the use of the more complex techniques in your work or department?

Current health of the use and application of tools and techniques. Data collection tools such as control charts, run charts and check sheets that comprise techniques (such as SPC) are generally used for monitoring and evaluation purposes. For continuous improvements, measurements are more difficult to define, and very often outputs can misrepresent the situation, or may even fail to reach any form of conclusion. In these circumstances, it is important to determine how to set measurable parameters, by whom, and what steps are usually taken after analysis or interpretation. The questions asked will be dictated by the job the individual is doing and his or her level in the organizational hierarchy.

Typical questions are:

- What are the expectations of the outcomes for the use of tools and techniques?
- Are they realistic?
- Do they reflect the true situation?
- Has there ever been any 'fudging' of data, so that a better picture is presented than is actually the case?
- Is more expected from the use of tools and techniques than can be delivered?
- Does this affect the subsequent use of tools and techniques?

Management

A major difficulty faced by an organization when embracing the principles of TQM is the issue of commitment and support of TQM by management, from senior managers down to first-line supervisors. Management style becomes an important issue, since this can vary from department to department and is very much dependent upon the personalities of the people involved. As before, the individuals themselves, their jobs and their status will dictate the level of questions.

Typical questions are:

- Does senior management support the use of tools and techniques?
- Are they committed to TQM?
- Is there any conflict between TQM and the short-term goals and objectives of the organization?
- Does the overall management style support and encourage worker involvement and empowerment?

Management knowledge of tools and techniques.   Often difficulties arise due to unrealistic expectations of the outcomes from the use and application of tools and techniques, a misconception about their achievable benefits, or even lack of experience and knowledge of the processes in the department or function.
   Typical questions are:

- Is there a policy in place in your department with regard to tools and techniques?
- Does your manager expect you to use tools and techniques as part of your job?
- Are you ever asked to use a tool and technique that you know cannot be applied to the process and procedures in your department.
- Does your manager have first hand understanding of the processes and procedures used in your department.

Departmental Management styles and philosophies.   Many applications of tools and techniques require interdepartmental cooperation and interaction, but this may be limited because of existing work practices and attitudes. Similarly, if there are any individual 'blockers' to their use, they are usually to be found at junior to middle management levels.
   Typical questions are:

- Does your manager support the use of tools and technique in your department or function?
- Does your manager encourage you to take responsibility for the processes and procedures in your department?
- Has your manager ever stopped you from collecting data that is required for the use of tools and techniques?
- Have the results obtained during problem solving exercises, process monitoring etc. ever been used adversely against individuals?
- Does a blame culture exist within the organization and/or

department?
- Has any continuous improvement initiative ever been put on the 'back burner', because of other management or company demands?
- Are you encouraged to interact and share information with other departments and functions?
- Does your manager encourage interdepartmental/function interaction?

Communication. They way in which the policies and philosophies of the organization are communicated is often reflected at the micro level of tools and techniques, as is the communications between hierarchical layers and between departments.
Typical questions are:

- How is quality-related information shared between departments and functions.
- Are you encourage to develop internal customer/supplier relationships.
- How good are interdepartmental communications.
- Is there good interaction between function and departments.

Resources

The aim of TQM is to produce flatter, leaner, more efficient organizations, but this cannot occur without the utilization of available resources (i.e. money, people, facilities, technology, time). This can affect the use and application of tools and techniques in a number of different ways.

People. Even with the use and application of technology, the backbone of any organization is its workforce. It is they who, by their very actions, add to the effectiveness of tools and techniques, and they themselves are subject to many influences.
Typical questions are:

- Are there sufficient people to participate in the problem solving and continuous improvement process?
- Is there sufficient people to sustain the use of tools and techniques, in terms of facilitators and mentor?.
- Is there an adequate management resource to drive the use and

application of tools and techniques?

- Are employees released, without difficulty, to attend training sessions (quality or other forms of training)?
- Does the workplace environment encourage the use and application of tools and techniques as part of normal working activities?
- Do the workforce feel secure about the future of the plant?
- Are the workforce motivated to continuously improve the activities for which they are responsible?

Data Collection and Analysis.   Typical questions are:

- Are adequate facilities provide for the collection and presentation of data (e.g. rulers, calculators, workbenches)?
- Are the facilities close enough to the working area?
- Are there sufficient facilities for everyone?
- Is there sufficient time to collect and analyse the data?
- Is there a need to collect the data?
- Do people know why data is being collected?
- Are they involved in its analysis?
- Are they encouraged to take responsibility for the results and the implementation of a course of action?

Change.   It should always be borne in mind that collecting data, analysis and improvement activities do not necessarily mean that change will occur.
    Typical questions are:

- Are there sufficient funds available to implement change that has resulted from the improvement or problem solving process?
- Is there a need for change?
- Are the individuals likely to be affected by the change involved in the decision making process?
- Who else is involved in the decision making process for change?
- Has the need for change ever been denied?
- Is there competition for resources between functions and departments?
- Is the information technology adequate to cope with the demands of some of the more complex tools and techniques?
- Are there adequate data presentation facilities?
- Is provision made for the coordination of collected data?

Education

There are very large differences in the educational levels of work-forces throughout European organizations. Similarly, there are different skill levels available to employers, particularly at craft and intermediate levels. This has a direct bearing on how the workforce should be educated to suit the demanding requirements of modern technology and methods of manufacture. Many of the issues and difficulties associated with tools and techniques have their origins in education, where basic literacy and numeracy are not of an adequate standard. Therefore, an essential task during the assessment is to establish some form of profile regarding the workforce skills of the organization.

Typical questions are:

- At what age did they leave school?
- Did they study for any examinations while at school?
- What qualifications did they acquire at school?
- Did they go on to any further education prior to starting work?
- Have they continued their education since leaving school and starting work?
- Do they feel that their mathematical and statistical knowledge is sufficient to meet the needs of their job?
- Do they feel that their language and communication skills are sufficient to meet the needs of their job?
- Do they feel that they have a problem understanding the basic concepts of tools and techniques?
- Is there anyone available to act as a coach and counsellor if these basic skills and knowledge are inadequate?

Training

Training is an essential element of TQM. For an organization it should provide a platform for enhancing its workforce skills and therefore its ultimate competitiveness in the global market-place. At an individual employee level, it should provide a focus for personal development and job satisfaction. There is a fine balance in satisfying the needs of both the organization and the individual, since meeting the needs of one may neglect the needs of the other.

Organizational quality training: policies and strategies. Typical questions are:

- Is there a quality training strategy?
- Is there any conflict between quality-related training and other training requirements?
- How are the quality training goals defined?
- Does the organization have the capabilities of providing the necessary training?
- Does quality training policies conflict with other policies and strategies?
- Are there defined strategies for TQM-related training?
- What role has the quality management system played in determining the training policies?
- How are the training requirements determined?

Organization training requirements and needs.   Typical questions are:

- Are the workforce skills assessed in any way?
- What means are there for evaluating the effectiveness of training?
- Has an audit of training effectiveness taken place?
- What steps are taken for monitoring the outcome of individual training events?
- To what degree is the training undertaken in a 'sheep dipping' mode?
- Have the effects of this method of mass training ever been evaluated?
- What is the role of the manager in post-training implementation?

Individual training.   Typical questions are:

- Has the individual received any company-specific quality-related training? What did it consist of and how was it delivered?
- Do they understand why they are receiving or have received quality training?
- Has the individual found the training useful?
- Has it made any difference to their job?
- What mix of people attended the training sessions. Did the mix aid or hinder the training event?
- Is there post-training backup and support?

- Have they been able to apply what they have learnt in the training to their own job?
- Have they experienced any difficulty in getting to the training event?

References

Akao, Y. 1991: *Quality Function Deployment: integrating customer requirements in product design*. Productivity Press, Massachusetts: Productivity
Press.

Anon. 1993: Customer service can reap rich rewards. *Strategic Insights into
Quality*, 1(1), 13–15.

Barker, T. B. 1990: *Engineering Quality by Design*. New York: Marcel Dekker.

Baumard, P. 1996: Organizations in the fog: an investigation into the dynamics of knowledge. In B. Moingeon and A. Edmonson (eds), Sage.
Organizational Learning and Competitive Advantage, London: Sage.

Bendell, A. T., Disney, J. and Pridmore, W. A. 1989: *Taguchi Methods:
Application in World Industry*. Bedford: IFS.

Benneyan, J. C. and Chute, A. D. 1993: SPC, process improvement and the
Deming PDCA circle in freight administration. *Production and Inventory
Management Journal*, 1st quarter, 35–40.

Bierhof, H. and Prais, S. J. 1993: Britain's skills and the school-teaching of
practical subjects: comparisons with Germany, the Netherlands and
Switzerland. *National Institute of Economic Review*, May, 55–73.

Booth, A. L. 1991: Job-related formal training: who receives it and what is it
worth? *Oxford Bulletin of Economics and Statistics*, 53(3), 281–94.

Bramley, P. and Kitson, B. 1994: Evaluating training against business criteria. *Journal of European Industrial Training*, 18(1), 10–14.

BS.6143, 1990: *Guide to the Economics of Quality*, Part 2, Prevention,
Appraisal and Failure Model. London: British Standards Institution.

BS.6143, 1992: *Guide to the Economics of Quality*, Part 1, *Process Cost Model*.
London: British Standards Institution.

BS EN ISO 8402, 1995: *Quality Management and Quality Assurance –
Vocabulary*. London: British Standards Institution.

Camp, R. C. 1989: *Benchmarking: the search for industry best practice that
leads to superior performance*. Milwaukee, Wisconsin: ASQC Quality Press.

Currie, R. M. 1989: *Work Study*. London: Pitman.

Dale, B. G. 1994: *Managing Quality*, 2nd edn. London: Prentice Hall.

Dale, B. G. and Cooper, C. L. 1992: *Total Quality and Human Resources: an
executive guide*. Oxford: Blackwell.

Dale, B. G., Huke, I. and Tonge, P. 1997: *Statistical Process Control*, Quality Booklet series, no. 9.Hong Kong Government Industry Department.

Dale, B. G. and Plunkett, J. J. 1995: *Quality Costing*, 2nd edn. London: Chapman & Hall.

Dale, B. G. and Shaw, P. 1990: Failure mode and effects analysis in the UK motor industry: a state-of-the-art study. *Quality and Reliability Engineering International*, 6(3), 179–88.

Dale, B. G. and Shaw, P. 1991: Statistical process control: an examination of common queries. *International Journal of Production Economics*, 22(1), 33–41.

Dale, B. G., Boaden, R. E. and Wilcox, M. 1993a: Quality management tool and technique classification, working paper no. 11, EPSRC GR/H/21499, Quality Management Centre, Manchester School of Management, UMIST.

—— 1993b: Difficulties encountered in the use of quality management tools and techniques, working paper no. 2, EPSRC GR/H/21499, Quality Management Centre, Manchester School of Management, UMIST.

Dale, B. G., Boaden, R. J. and Lascelles, D. M. 1994: Total quality management: an overview. In B.G. Dale (ed.), *Managing Quality*, 2nd edn. London: Prentice Hall.

Dale, B. G., Boaden, R. J., Wilcox, M. and McQuater, R. E. 1997: The use of quality management tools and techniques: an examination of some key issues. International journal of technology management. in press.

Easton, G. S. and Jarrell, S. L. 1996: The effects of total quality management on corporate performance: an empirical investigation. *Journal of Business*, 14(4), 16–31.

Eureka, W. L. and Ryan, N. E. 1988: *The Customer Driven Company – Managerial Perspectives on Quality Function Deployment*. Dearborn: Michigan: ASI Press.

Ford Motor Company, 1988: *Potential Failure Mode and Effects Analysis: an instruction manual*. Brentwood: Ford Motor Company.

—— 1991: *Quality Methods Handbook*. Brentwood: Ford Motor Company.

Ishikawa, K. 1976: *Guide to Quality Control*. Tokyo: Asian Productivity Organization.

Juran, J. M. 1988: *Quality Control Handbook*, 4th edn. New York: McGraw-Hill.

Kane, V. E. 1989: *Defect Prevention: use of simple statistical tools*. New York: Marcel Dekker.

Kano, N., Taraka, H. and Yamaga, Y. 1983: *The TQC Activity of Deming Prize Recipients and its Economic Impact*. Tokyo: Union of Japanese Scientists and Engineers.

Larry, L. 1993: Betting to win on the Baldrige winners. *Business Week*, 18 October, 16–17.

Lascelles, D. M. and Dale, B. G. 1993: *The Road to Quality*. Beadford: IFS.

Letza, S. R., Zairi, M. and Whymark, J. 1997: TQM – fad or tool for sustainable competitive advantage: an empirical study of the impact of TQM on bottom line business results, University of Bradford Management Centre, Bradford.

Lewis, L. 1984: *Quality Improvement Handbook. Hampshire:* IBM.

Lochnar, R. H. and Matar, J. E. 1990: *Designing for Quality*. London: Chapman & Hall.

Mason, G. and Wagner, K. 1994: High level skills and industrial competitiveness: post graduate engineers and scientists in Britain and Germany, Report Series No. 6. National Institute of Economic and Social Research.

Mason, G., van Ark, B. and Wagner, K. 1994: Productivity and workforce skills: food processing in four european countries. *National Institute Economic Review*, February, 62–83.

McNair, C. J. and Leibfreid, K. 1993: *Benchmarking: a tool for continuous improvement*. London: HarperCollins.

McQuater, R. E., Dale B. G., Wilcox, M. and Boaden, R. J. 1994: The Effectiveness of quality management techniques and tools in the continuous improvement process: an examination. In *Proceedings of Factory 2000 – Advances in Factory Automation*, Conference Publication No. 398, IEE, October, pp. 574–80.

McQuater, R. E., Wilcox, M., Dale B. G. and Boaden, R. J. 1995: Issues and difficulties with quality management techniques and tools: implications for education and training. In *Proceedings of the 31st MTDR Conference*, Manchester: UMIST, pp. 159–64.

McQuater, R. E., Dale, B. G., Boaden, R. J. and Wilcox, M. 1996: The effectiveness of quality management tools and techniques: an examination of the key influences in five plants. *Proceedings of the Institution of Mechanical Engineers*, 210(B4: 329–39.

Mehrman, M. I. and Harris, M. S. 1993: The synergy of modern management. *Bobbin*, 3(8), 64–9.

Mizuno, S. 1988: *Management for Quality Improvement, the Seven New Q.C. Tools*. Cambridge, Massachusetts: Productivity Press.

Montgomery, D. C. 1991: *Introduction to Statistical Quality Control*, 2nd edn. New York: John Wiley.

National Westminster Bank 1987: *Quality Service Action Teams: Team Member Manual*. London: National Westminster Bank, Quality Services Department.

Oakland, J. S. 1993: *Total Quality Management*, 2nd edn. London: Heinemann.

Oakland, J. S. 1997: *Statistical Process Control: a practical guide*, 3rd edn. London: Heinmann.

Owen, M. 1989: *SPC and Continuous Improvement*. Bedford: IFS.

Ozeki, K. and Asaka, T. 1990: *Handbook of Quality Tools*. Cambridge, Massachusetts: Productivity Press.

Plackett, R. L. and Burmann, J. P. 1946: The design of optimum multi-factorial experiments. *Bionsetrika*, 33(3), 305–25.

Prais, S. J. 1993: Economic performance and education: the nature of Britain's deficiencies, Discussion Paper No. 52, National Institute of Economic and Social Research.

Price, F. 1984: *Right First Time*. Aldershot: Gower Press.

Reimann, C. 1995: Quality proves to be a good investment. *US Department of Commerce News*, 3 February.

Shingo, S. 1986: *Zero Quality Control: source inspection and the poka-yoke system*. Massachusetts: Productivity Press.

Skorstad, E. 1994: Lean production, conditions of work and worker commitment. *Economic and Industrial Democracy*, 15, 429–55.

Smithers, A. and Robinson, P. 1991: *Beyond Compulsory Schooling, A Numerical Picture*. London: The Council for Industry and Higher Education.

Steedman, H., Mason, G. and Wagner, K. 1991: Intermediate skills in the work place: deployment, standards and supply in Britain, France and Germany. *National Institute Economic Review*, May, 60–76.

Taguchi, G. 1986: *Introduction to Quality Engineering.* Tokyo: Asian Productivity Organization.

United States Department of Commerce, 1995: *Quality Management Proves to be a Good Investment.* Washington, DC: National Institute of Standards and Technology.

United States General Accounting Office, 1991: Management Practices: US Companies Improve Performance through Quality Efforts, Report to the Honorable Donald Ritter, House of Representatives, May.

Watson, G. H. 1992: *The Benchmarking Workbook: Adapting Best Practices for Performance Improvement.* Cambridge, Massachusetts: Productivity Press.

Wilcox, M., Dale, B. G., Boaden, R. J. and McQuater, R. E. 1994: Harmonisation: can TQM be successfully integrated with other policies? In *Proceedings of the British Academy of Management*, Lancaster, 12–14 September 1994, abstract, pp. 362–3.

Wisner, J. D. and Eakins, S. G. 1994: Competitive assessment of the Baldrige winners. *International Journal of Quality and Reliability Management*, 11(2), 8–25.

Wolf, A. 1993: *Failure in Reform in Mathematics Education: the case of engineering*, National Institute Briefing Note No. 5. London: National Institute of Economic and Social Research.

Index

Printed and bound by CPI Group (UK) Ltd, Croydon, CR0 4YY

23/04/2025

14660955-0004